ATTRACT

ATTRACT

4 Simple Steps to Engaging Your
Ideal Client with Zero Prospecting

JOSH SCHOENLY

ATTRACT

*4 Simple Steps to Engaging Your
Ideal Client with Zero Prospecting*

ISBN   978-1-61961-481-9   *Paperback*
         978-1-61961-482-6   *Ebook*

LIONCREST
PUBLISHING

To Pam and our four beautiful children: Kaden, Kole, Sammy, and Teagan. Thank you for your continued support and encouragement. You are and will continue to be my inspiration. Love you all so much!

Contents

. . . . .

Introduction

· · · · ·

It felt like I was having a nightmare. But it was real.

There I was, putting the "for sale" sign in the yard of my own house. I didn't want to leave, but I had to. I was dead broke.

"It's going to be okay, Josh," my mother-in-law told me. "You two and the kids can live with us for as long as you need to."

I felt like I'd failed in every way imaginable. How had this happened? Nobody worked harder than I did when it came to real estate sales. Nobody.

And yet, there I was broke, thousands of dollars in debt,

and about to move in with my in-laws. I was being forced to sell the house that my family and I loved.

It was humiliating.

And in retrospect, it was exactly what needed to happen for me to understand the true path to success in real estate.

I'm about to show you how a select few realtors on the planet are successful, while most realtors are struggling to survive. I know the secrets of the successful agents because I became one myself, and now I help others achieve the same success.

But first, let's take a step back in time. Let's look at how it all went wrong for me and how it's still going wrong for the majority of people in real estate sales. We have to understand what the problem is before we fully understand the solutions.

HOW IT ALL BEGAN

Real estate is a form of direct sales, and my first introduction to direct sales was a network marketing company. I'd joined the company through a friend's referral, and I was initially excited about the opportunity.

My excitement quickly changed to skepticism and frustration. After I got signed up and was officially labeled a "distributor," I was told to write down the names and numbers of two hundred people, and at that moment, I realized that wasn't the way I envisioned building a business.

I could certainly envision the end results of a successful business and the full picture that the company was painting for those who could follow their traditional plan, take action, and do the work. So I tried my best to do that initial exercise.

I wrote down a few names, but when I got to the thirteenth or fourteenth name, I realized it was complete nonsense. I didn't want to call my friends and family, or two hundred distant acquaintances, even if the product I was selling would truly add value to their lives.

Soon after, I can vividly remember getting calls and e-mails from people who were clearly doing a similar exercise for their network marketing companies. It wasn't anything I asked for, or sought out myself. I learned how terrible it was to be sold things in that fashion as a consumer.

At that point in my life, I decided that I didn't want to build a business that way. I decided that I would figure out how to attract people to me versus trying to chase them.

It took me many years to accomplish this feat and to get to a point where I consider myself an expert who is very qualified to write this book. I'm still learning and growing every day in order to help other people accomplish it for themselves. It's a set of skills that has provided me a much higher income than I ever could have imagined, and it's given me a peace of mind that drives my confident optimism for today and toward tomorrow.

In the earliest days of my entrepreneurial path, there were many sleepless nights. There was a burning in the pit of my stomach and an anxiety that came from wondering where money was going to come from. I wondered how we were going to make our next mortgage payment, or pay any of our bills. It was terrible.

I wish I'd had this book back then. I wish I'd had access to the principles that we're going to outline here. These are the strategies that will help you thrive in real estate sales, but also in any other business venture you choose to be involved with in the future. These principles and methodologies can be applied universally.

In this book, we're going to focus on applying these strategies to real estate sales. Specifically, we'll be working toward the goal of attracting clients to you in a systematic fashion and being able to do so at will. Instead of begging, chasing, or seeking out clients, we'll focus on getting them to come to you. Instead of paying extremely high costs to lead vendors and relying upon them for your entire business, we'll focus on becoming self-reliant.

You'll learn to attract business to you in a predictable fashion, without needing to resort to any of those old and painful ways of doing things: cold-calling, prospecting, knocking on doors, or purchasing leads from lead vendors.

You're about to learn how to play an entirely different game.

Playing the traditional game is painful for most people. Admittedly, there might be a very small percentage of people out there who actually enjoy cold-calling and prospecting and door-knocking. But for most of us, it's very painful and uncomfortable to do those things because it's not how we want to be treated as a consumer.

Instead of taking the painful path and trying to play the same game that everybody else is playing, let's play a different game entirely. Let's change the paradigm completely and start attracting people to us.

You'll do that by providing value—the value that comes from being informative, being entertaining, and being different than all the other agents in your market.

HOW REAL ESTATE SALESPEOPLE ARE TYPICALLY MISLED

Agents often enter the world of real estate with misperceptions about how they're going to build a business. There really isn't any training provided by most brokers when it comes to actually building a business or more specifically marketing. That's because it's often just a numbers game to traditional brokers who bring in new agents.

Their thinking encompasses the following: How many agents can we get at the brokerage level? How many agents can we get at the national level? It's not about helping each agent to build a business and get to the end result that they were promised when they were recruited.

Most agents become an agent because they have some entrepreneurial aspirations. They have big dreams and want more from lives. They certainly don't dream of becoming a glorified telemarketer or door-to-door salesperson. If that's what the recruiters told new agents upfront, then no one would go through the time and effort of getting a license in the first place.

Traditionally, new agents are completely betrayed by what they're promised when they're recruited. It's a bait and switch. Prospective agents will be told they can live their ideal lifestyles. Their incomes will be limitless. They're going to have all this time freedom and a happy career.

But when it comes time to do the actual work, every-thing changes.

Now they're expecting you to do the things they con-veniently forgot to tell you about. The cold-calling, door-knocking, or maybe the writing down of names of two hundred distant acquaintances to call.

And what's their advice if you're not doing enough deals? Well, you've just got to pound on the phones more, they'll tell you. Come in earlier, maybe at nine in the morning, and just make more cold calls. Just keep mindlessly pound-ing away.

Who wants that? Do you get excited when your phone rings and a salesperson is on the other end?

We've reverse engineered all of this. You won't have to chase people. You'll get them calling you, e-mailing you, texting you, and wanting you to help them.

This is more important than most people realize. The great marketer Gary Vaynerchuk once said that *how* you make money is more important than actually making the money. There's a lot of truth to that.

You can make money in real estate by cold-calling,

door-knocking, and all the other painful nonsense. What I would suggest though is to think about these approaches by answering the following questions:

- Is this an approach you can sustain long term?
- Do you want to sustain it? (In other words, is it something you could get excited about doing for years?)
- Is this something your potential clients want?

You especially have to think about it from the consumer experience, because you're going to need them to refer you to their friends and family. Who's going to be more likely to refer you to their friends: a person you attracted to you (in a way that was pleasurable to them), or a person you relentlessly chased until they just gave up and chose you out of submission? Where are you going to get more of the repeat customers and referrals that are crucial to surviving in the real estate business?

If you acquire your clients in a way that is unappealing to them, they are dramatically less likely to send you more business. If their first impression of you was that of the relentless hound dog, that's never going to leave their minds. You never get a second chance to make your first impression. You might be able to get referrals through the same bludgeoning of people, but for 99.9 percent of us, that is not an enjoyable, sustainable, or effective process.

Compare this to the opposite approach. If your clients' first impression of you was that you provided great value—whether it was being informative, entertaining, knowledgeable, or just interesting—then referring you becomes an afterthought. In fact, they'll go out of their way to refer your business and become an advocate for you!

It's a forgone conclusion. They're going to send other people to you. Why? They want to provide value to their friends and family, and they see you as valuable.

That's the approach you want to take, and the one we'll walk through in this book.

WHAT ABOUT BUYING LEADS WHO HAVE EXPRESSED INTEREST ONLINE?

Lead vendors are everywhere in the real estate industry. I personally classify them as pirates, hijackers, and kidnappers. They advertise that these are new leads, people who are interested in speaking with you, but essentially these lead vendors are using your listings to generate leads and then selling those leads back to you. They steal your ship to go find your treasure and then sell it back to you.

With Zillow and Trulia and Realtor.com, in my opinion, they're taking your listings and the business that you've generated, and they're syndicating them through various ways. They then use that asset (which is really your asset), leverage some technology to intercept the leads that would've come to you, and then sell those leads back to you. And if you're not paying them for those leads, then the leads that came from your listing might go to someone else.

The worst part about it is that the agent who buys your leads may provide terrible service. He or she may not return the client's phone calls, or may not have the client's best interest in mind. And all that does is creates a negative reputation of real estate agents in general.

You may be the most ethical, caring, and thoughtful agent in the world, but when the lead vendors hijack your listings, you don't have a chance to prove it to the people who are interested in your listing. That is unless, of course, you pay the lead vendors' outrageous fee to be the "featured state agent" in your zip code. Then you'll get your own leads.

I'll show you how to get your leads to come directly to you instead of being unknowingly lured into the grasp of the lead vendors.

THE TWO VILLAINS OF THIS STORY

There are really two villains in this story of traditional real estate: lead vendors and the painful, traditional brokerage mentality. The traditional mentality asks you to take all the wrong actions and then guilts you with the feeling that, if you're not succeeding, there must be something wrong with you—that you must need more accountability, or to make more cold calls, or require more "coaching," etc.

In both cases—lead vendors and traditional brokerage mentality—there's zero affinity built with the customer. They don't know you. They may request information about a property, and they may even be serious about buying, but what's your positioning when you call them?

It's still you, a stranger, chasing them. "Hi there, Mr. Prospect. My name is Josh with XYZ Realty, and I see that you requested information about the property at 123 Main Street." You have to explain who you are, why you're calling, and figure out whether the customer is truly motivated to take action.

Even though the consumer in that case is taking action by requesting more information, most agents trained by these old-school brokers follow up like hound dogs. Most of the time the consumer just wants a little bit of information, maybe it's the school district or number of bedrooms. But the agents hound the prospects relentlessly for more information and won't let go until the person ultimately hangs up.

There are some agents who are successful with purchased leads, but it still goes back to that Gary V quote: how you get the business is as important as actually getting the business. And with lead vendors, they often will sell that lead to more than one agent. They're rarely exclusive leads. So you've got to call that lead before all the other agents do.

This is the point where your career becomes exactly the opposite of the freedom you were promised when you were being recruited to be an agent. It means that you're sitting at the dinner table with your family and your phone buzzes because you just got a lead. You know that if you don't call that person within ten minutes, somebody else is going to get it.

Here you are, sitting at the dinner table with your kids and spouse and you've got to think to yourself, what am I going to do here? Because I know if I walk away to take this call, I know what I'm coming back to. But I've got my broker's voice in the back of my head saying, "You've just got to work harder. You've got to be on call every hour of every day."

No wonder there's such a high burnout rate of real estate agents. *This is absolute nonsense.*

In the process that we're going to walk through, your first interaction with consumers (your potential clients) will be completely the opposite of this scenario. There will already be an affinity built between you and a prospective customer by the time that person reaches out to you by e-mail, text, or phone. You will already have built some rapport with them, and because of that, you can return their inquiry at a time that's convenient to you.

If you've already built affinity and rapport with people by leveraging the strategies and tactics in this book, you can call clients back the next day if that's more convenient for you. Why? Because that person has already decided that they're going to be your client. And they decided that because you're different than the other agents.

In the traditional brokerage mentality where you're just chasing people, you are simply a commodity. And you feel like one. I never want to feel that I'm a commodity, and you shouldn't either. That's because not only does it feel terrible, but commodities only go down in price and value over time.

If you're doing that traditional stuff, you're acknowledging that you're willing to be a commodity. And that's a terrible place to be. When you're the commodity, it's a downward spiral into oblivion.

You buy a lead, get the notification on your phone, and call back thirty minutes later, only to hear the lead say, "I'm sorry. Bob Smith at XYZ Realty called us first, so we're going to work with him." With the traditional method you simply have commodity agents battling other commodity agents for mediocre customers.

But when you're a person who has already built an affinity with customers by delivering value, it's the exact opposite. It's happened over and over to me, as well as to my clients. The customer, on his or her first contact with you, says something like this: "Hi, Josh, this is Jennifer Jones. You don't know me, but I feel like I know you already. I've been getting your e-mails and videos and market reports for a year or two. I'm now ready to sell my home, and I'd like to know what the next step is toward getting it listed with you."

See the difference? You've done nothing in this interaction so far, but the customer has already decided to give you his or her business. And that's because at this point, you've already done a lot of things that provided value to that person and positioned you as a helpful authority in his or her mind. You've built up a "bank of goodwill" with the customer, even though that person hasn't actually met you yet!

When you are attracting customers to you, it means there's a different positioning going on. They already view you as the expert or "the authority" and as someone who cares about them as clients, even though they have never actually talked to you previously.

You can absolutely accomplish this. I'm not going to tell you that it will always be easy. It does require some work. But it will definitely be easier than making one hundred cold calls every day, or knocking on twenty strangers' doors every day, or spending thousands of dollars every month buying your own leads from the lead vendor pirates.

In fact, the old methods are so difficult that it takes psychological miracles to get through the process on a daily basis. Why do traditional brokers and sales trainers have all these "pump you up" routines before they make cold calls? Because they know that cold calls are completely deflating to a human being. I know because I have years of experience doing those types of calls. It's an absolutely terrible experience, every single time.

I call myself "productively lazy." I want to be as productive as possible, but I'm still pretty lazy in a way that other people call efficient. I remember calling a few of the leads I bought in my early years when I was involved in the network marketing company. I hated it so much that I could only call five or ten people a week, and I was always praying that they wouldn't answer the phone.

I was hoping they wouldn't answer so I could just say, "Well, I made ten calls and nobody answered. It's not my fault. I did what I was supposed to." That entire process, from my thoughts to the actions I had to take, would suck the life out of me.

The conversations with prospective customers, when they happened, felt terrible. I knew it was not how a natural, healthy business conversation should go. This cannot be the way to do things, I'd think to myself, before and after the calls.

Later, after I mastered the methods in this book, I was able to enjoy a completely different experience. The conversations would begin with a new voice at the other end of the line calling me in a happy and enthusiastic tone. "Hey, this is Bill. I've been getting your e-mails and watching your videos. I found a property that I'm interested in. What do we need to do next?"

That's the difference. It's like getting an unexpected check in the mail versus getting an unexpected bill in the mail. It's a completely opposite event, with a completely opposite feeling generated by it.

I want you to get the positive event and the positive feelings that come as a result. What happens to you in the course of selling real estate, or any business, is going to have an effect on how you feel as a person. And how you feel as a person will affect what you attract into your life.

Part of this process is making yourself a more attractive person. I don't mean physically, as in your hair or eyes or skin, but I mean overall attractiveness. When you understand these skills and experience the positive results and feelings, you will find yourself feeling more attractive.

You'll feel more attractive because you will be.

You'll have a confidence about you. There will be an aura about you that is different because you're not doing the stuff you hate doing. You're not selling your soul to the devil, or doing things that cost you self-esteem, just because you were told you had to do those things by a traditional broker, trainer, coach, or "guru."

Instead, you're providing value. You're being interesting

and entertaining, and you're appreciated by people. You feel attractive. And that's because you are.

MY EARLY EXPERIENCES IN REAL ESTATE

Before I got my real estate license, I was buying and selling real estate personally. I was in real estate as an active investor using these same principles to attract motivated sellers, tenants, and buyers.

That was the initial breakthrough and epiphany for me. You can read about other people's success in attracting people to them, but then when you're able to start doing it yourself, you have a different level of belief. It becomes a different level of understanding and belief.

When I followed these principles, I began to build assets that had significant equity. The mailing list and e-mail database that I had built were not only helping me to sell properties, but I was monetizing the list in other ways as well.

Through continually seeking knowledge and wanting to learn, I found a fellow who had a client attraction system for building a real estate practice. It was focused primarily on attracting local real estate investors, and it really resonated with me because it was very similar to what I was already doing, but it was more scalable.

It was more of a real business model. What I'd been doing was more like opportunity-focused approach versus an actual systematic business system. I'd been building these assets, but I still had to figure out how to put deals together. It was easier than cold-calling and prospecting, because I did have these assets, but it still wasn't really systematic in its approach. That is, until I found this fellow's work.

As a result, I got my real estate license for very different reasons than most people get into real estate. I did it so I could apply this marketing system. Most people get their license first and then figure out how to acquire clients and how to sell. I did the opposite, which gave me a different perspective and a big advantage.

Over the course of time, I was masterminding and networking with people around the world who were applying this system in their local markets. Along the way, I realized that I was really passionate about helping people improve their businesses and lives through this system. I love to teach and coach people on these powerful marketing techniques and to see my clients achieve amazing results.

MY RESULTS IN THE WORLD OF REAL ESTATE SALES

When it comes to selling real estate, I rose to the top quickly. I was number one in sales in my brokerage in only my second year as an agent. I was following this proven system, applying my own experience and knowledge, and taking action according to the feedback loops I received from my local market.

Everything worked so well that I got to a point where I became completely flooded with customers. I realized that I'd either need to hire a team to continue growing my real estate sales, or pull back on that and focus on the thing I am more passionate about: helping other agents.

I certainly can help homebuyers find a home that's a great fit for them, and it's an enjoyable process. But I know that real estate agents need me more, and I'm obsessively passionate about helping them solve their biggest problems in marketing.

Many agents are out there right now thinking, "How do I get new clients? What can I do so that I'm not waking up every morning wondering where my next commission check will come from? How am I going to pay my bills?"

Those are scary thoughts. I know, because there was a time I had them myself.

I want to help agents answer those questions and build a better life for themselves. That's my passion and the reason I'm writing this book.

A DECADE OF EVOLUTION AND EXPERIENCE

I've now been helping real estate professionals and employing these techniques for nearly ten years. Over those years, tens of thousands of real estate agents have participated in various programs and trainings of mine and are subscribers to the principles and methodologies that I teach and believe in.

In my years of testing different channels to deliver value to my subscribers, one of the things that I've realized was I could broaden the reach of the impact by looking at new ways of reaching people. I didn't need a company with more resources to purchase my content and distribute it. Instead, I just needed to look differently at the situation and how I distribute content myself.

That's how I was able to write this book, and I've launched a podcast ("The Client Alchemist Show"), as well as an entirely new brand (**ClientAlchemist.com**). Utilizing new channels of distribution, while still applying the same time-tested marketing methodologies, has been a renewed confirmation of what my purpose and mission are. The successful approach has evolved over time because consumer behavior is changing, and we're changing with it.

I'm undertaking these new and innovative projects because I want to help more people. There were many failures and learnings along the way. These temporary obstacles made me rethink everything, and in the end, they helped me to crystallize my purpose and mission. They forced me to think differently about how to get this message out to as many agents as possible, and this book is one of those ways.

THE "SECOND MOVER" ADVANTAGE

In the world of technology and business, there's a term called "second mover advantage." It means, quite simply, that the second mover in a market has an advantage over the first mover. You'll get that second mover advantage through this book and through our website because we were the first movers who endured all the trial and error to arrive at the strategies that work.

In our new brand and service, which is called Client Alchemist Pro, we'll be continuing all kinds of testing and experimenting for our community. We'll be on the cutting edge of all the newest technologies and techniques, and we'll endure a lot of failure on the path toward repeatedly finding the successful and dependable methods that we'll recommend to our community.

By reading this book, and being part of our community, you won't have to be the trailblazer. The trailblazers get burned and expend a ton of energy clearing the path. It's the first person after the trailblazer who has the easier path to success. That's the second mover and that's where the advantage is found: learning from the failures of the initial innovators, but still being one of the first people on the new path.

As strategies evolve, we will too. That's how we've kept such a large following and community over the past decade, and why those people enjoy a powerful advantage over their local competition.

HOW FAST WILL YOU SEE RESULTS?

One of the biggest challenges involved with the approach I'm about to outline is this: you'll need to be patient. You are going to have to suspend your disbeliefs and doubts for several weeks, take consistent action, and be okay with the fact that you may not see instant results.

Don't be discouraged if you're not seeing immediate results, but then again, don't be surprised if you do experience some immediate positive effects.

In the long term, you're going to build powerful assets that are easy to maintain. The problem with the old-school way is that all of its approaches are short term in focus, and you have to forever be building and rebuilding your business. You can't stop, ever.

But if you do what we outlined here, you can create assets, e-mail databases, fan bases, phone databases, and other long-term assets that you can leverage indefinitely. And most importantly, it will bring people to you, instead of you chasing them.

Both of these methods are going to be hard work. It's hard work taking the traditional path and doing things that create a daily misery for you—things that you'll have to sustain forever and endure every day.

It's also hard work to take the actions I'll recommend and to have complete faith that they will bring the results that you've never experienced before. But this hard path, for most people, will be infinitely more pleasurable and provide you with the freedom and peace of mind that you're looking for.

There's no easy button, no bullshit "fast-track" nonsense. That's what the lead vendors promise and what traditional brokers might promise. But I won't promise you that, because it's not true. There is no fast track. This will take consistent work, patience, faith, and persistence.

However, I will promise you this: it's worth it.

THE PARADIGM SHIFT YOU NEED TO EMBRACE: YOUR NEW JOB FUNCTION

Let's get started on your new mind-set. Your paradigm shift begins now.

You sell real estate, and you're good at it. You likely tell people that you're a real estate agent, and that's technically true. But for the remainder of this book, I want you to think of yourself as something different: a publisher.

Start looking at your business as a publishing company, or media company—a publishing company that also happens to sell real estate. When you have that mind-set and focus, you can control the perception people have about you and your brand.

Part of the process that we're about to undertake is to identify the audience you want: the audience you want to communicate with, be a part of, and attract to you. Then, from the publishing and media side, you'll determine how you are going to create content that is valuable to that audience.

You're going to create value through content with no

explicit expectation for that audience to do business with you. There will be no chasing, no begging, and no pandering, because this won't be about you.

It will be about *them*.

That's the central theme of this paradigm shift, which will change your business and your life for the better. You'll be a publisher creating value for the audience of your choosing, and it will be 100 percent about *them*.

Think about it for a moment: who is the focus of the message if I am doing traditional advertising, or cold-calling, or knocking on doors? It's me, me, me. It is me first and then the customer second, or not at all in most cases. Now, as a publisher who creates value for your customers, you'll be putting *them* first.

Most consumers view real estate agents as a necessary evil for buying or selling real estate, like an annoying pest. But this perception will change if you publish valuable content for the audience that you want to help and serve. When this shift occurs, you'll attract that audience to you, and you'll be viewed as a welcome guest in the real estate transaction.

It's a shift from annoying pest to welcome guest. That's the difference.

The customers will think, "This is someone who has earned the right to be a valuable part of this transaction versus somebody I have to use because they have the keys to the castle, or the secret forms that we have to use, or the actual MLS access." It's a completely different perspective in the eyes of your target customers.

If you can deliver that kind of value to them, you can build a massive amount of goodwill with them.

It's also a big part of how you'll build the type of assets that have lasting equity. When a real estate agent retires (for those lucky enough to be able to retire), if they have a business they want to sell, they're really just selling their database. If you change your business approach to focusing on building that asset, and developing goodwill and strong relationships with the people inside that database, you will have an incredibly valuable asset to sell in the end.

But much more importantly than the endgame of selling your business and retiring, this path will lead you to an enjoyable and lucrative career in real estate sales.

CHAPTER ONE

How to Escape the Real Estate Rat Race

· · · · ·

In the world of real estate sales, there are no retirement plans. There are no pension plans and no way to exit with a profit. That's one of the primary reasons that it's so important to shift the paradigm toward a different way of thinking and doing business in this industry.

One of the things that I see and hear often from older real estate agents is that they have to keep selling and keep working longer than they want to because they don't have a backup plan, and they don't have a way to exit the business.

When you build an audience and you create platforms, there are many opportunities to profit from your work with that audience, and it goes well beyond real estate transactions. This will become an asset for you that has real, actual equity to it.

HOW TO BUILD EQUITY IN WAYS THAT OTHER AGENTS DON'T

Most real estate agents run their businesses in a way that they build no equity of any kind. There's nothing that gives the actual business value, and if they stop selling, their income stops immediately. It drops off a cliff and goes away.

But when you build an audience and a platform to communicate with them, there are numerous ways to monetize that, which is what drives the ultimate value of your asset. One common way of monetizing your asset is to partner with other high-quality service providers who are looking to reach the same audience that you've already built. You can set up reciprocal relationships, cross-marketing, or even simply paid endorsements to expand into their platforms and yours.

I had a student a few years ago who built an audience locally and decided to move halfway across the country. Even though his audience could not go with him, he was able to monetize that asset and turn it into an income stream that he could keep for himself.

How did he do it? He partnered with an agent he liked and trusted and essentially leased the audience to that agent. This person was paying him a fee plus a percentage of all real estate sales that came from that audience.

If he was a typical agent, he would've lost everything when he moved away. All of the hard work and years of effort that had gone into building his business would have been gone because he was no longer physically present in that location.

But for him, because he applied the principles that are outlined in this book, he had a valuable asset that he could leverage from any location. If he was retiring instead of moving, it would've worked the same way.

Here's another story one of my students recently sent me:

Hey Josh, I have tons of good stories for you from applying the methods and principles you teach. I'm trying to keep it a little low key, as I know some realtors in my area have tried your techniques and given up on them. So I know they subscribe to you for sure.

Here is maybe the best story I can give you, as it's all encompassing.

I started real estate in 2010. The market was pretty low then, and I was fresh and ready to start. I had a rocky start, closing about eight deals in my first year. In 2011, I found you, or you found me, or a combination of those both with your marketing.

Since then I have grown to be the number one team agent in my area. I now have a big team. Four buyers' agents, a listing specialist, myself as the team leader, and two full-time assistants. We closed 220 deals in 2015, edging out the previous big dog in the market by about 15 deals. Our average sales price in my area is $272,000 for 2015. Your members can do the math on that one.

My main lead generation techniques are the ones you teach. I wrote you a long time ago about how I sat down one day and followed them step by step. I blotted out a huge chunk of a day, and did every step in a row, without taking a break. By the end of the day, I was already generating foreclosure leads.

Funny side story...I was generating so many leads so quickly that the real estate board called me in to talk about how that wasn't fair and that I must be doing something wrong/unethical. True story. In one of my e-mail blasts I said, "I'm excited to say that we have 800 people that have subscribed to my service..." Well another realtor from our board obviously was one of those people, and they complained that I was "marketing other brokerages' listings" by doing the foreclosure page. Of course, our board rules say we can do that...so nothing ever happened. They just didn't think it was fair that a new realtor was selling so much.

Anyway, I use your programs every day, and I have tweaked them to my own needs. Because of one I created (Free List of Just New Homes in Your Area), I have landed a total of 6 builders as clients over the years. One of those builders does 40 deals a year with me, and we have double ended a ton of those listings with your systems. They see that I am generating many leads, and they can get those leads if they hire me.

I know this is long, but I saw your post asking for stories. You have done nothing but boost my career and my entire lifestyle since we "met" in 2011. I owe you a big debt of gratitude. So I hope my stories can help you inspire all of our members.

— JUSTIN MYER

There are so many lessons and takeaways in Justin's story that I've actually included a bonus article you can find at **http://ClientAlchemist.com/BookExtras**.

When most agents hear the word audience or clientele, they're going to think I'm talking about the customers who have been in touch with the agent over the years. They've called, e-mailed, interacted, and maybe even purchased a property. But that's only one small piece of the audience you're about to build.

We're going to talk about an "invisible audience." I call it an invisible audience because it is a large group of people you can market to in a way that is almost invisible.

These are people who haven't even necessarily opted in for your e-mail communications, they haven't really called or texted you, and they haven't become a fan of your page. But they're consuming the content you create and still engaging with you from a distance. They're absolutely part of your audience, whether you know it or not.

I have a private client who's building an invisible audience of people who are interested in new construction homes in his market. This audience is an asset that he could leverage (either now or in the future) by partnering with a new home builder in his market. He has an audience and a communication platform that any home builder could benefit from.

How would this happen? The builder could give him property listings, or pay him to market and promote the home builder's properties. There are many, many different ways that this innovative agent can monetize his new construction audience.

And these opportunities only exist for him because he started thinking differently and applying the strategies we'll discuss in this book.

HOW NEW AGENTS NORMALLY FEEL ABOUT THE WORD "MARKETING"

Marketing can be an enjoyable, effective, critically important piece of daily life for a real estate agent. But in traditional real estate marketing, with brokers stuck in the old mind-set, marketing is absolutely not a happy thought for most agents.

The expectations are completely warped from the start, when agents are recruited. They have a beautiful picture of the opportunity in their heads, including the freedom of time, the limitless income opportunity, and all the other glorious platitudes that are painted for them. So they get their license and choose the brokerage with the happiest narrative.

Then the rug gets pulled out from under them.

Day one is when they're told it's time to get to work on marketing. And typically, it's all the painful and terrible things we talked about in the introduction. Glorified tele-marketing. Chasing. Begging.

So it's no surprise that most agents have a massive amount of resistance (consciously or unconsciously) to engaging in this type of "marketing." There's a resistance to a lot of it, because they've been browbeaten into believing that "marketing" means cold-calling, door-knocking, writing down two hundred names, and terrible things like that.

That's not marketing, to me. That's pestering. And that's the reason why the real estate industry is often dead last in reputation and satisfaction among consumers. It's because agents are told to pester people in this interruptive form of advertising their services, and in the end, it creates a negative aura around the real estate agent and the entire industry.

This is what creates the negative cycle that most agents are stuck in.

They don't want to do these pestering activities, and so there's a resistance to it. Then, since there are no other marketing ideas given to them by their brokers, the agents aren't generating business. They're barely getting by; they're living from commission check to commission check.

To make things worse, any time they ask for help from their broker or from the typical sales guru or coach, they're made to feel like they're broken. They'll get accusatory questions and statements like these:

- "Well, how many dials are you making? You just need to make more dials!"
- "How many doors are you knocking on every day?"
- "How many business cards are you handing out at networking functions?"
- "Have you asked your friends for introductions to their friends?"
- "You just gotta put your nose to the grindstone."

They make agents feel like it's their own fault, and it's the agent who is broken. But in reality, what's broken is the antiquated and ineffective methodologies that brokers are expecting of agents. It's so far outdated that it's not even remotely effective, and that's the reason why real estate agents have a massive negative reputation.

It becomes a zero-sum game. There's also this message

out there from traditional brokers and coaches that you've just got to grind it out for three months or six months or twelve months until you start getting some traction. But that's a lie.

When you build a business like that, the grind is never going to go away. Why? Because, as I mentioned in the introduction, how you get your clients is as important as getting the clients. And if you are getting your clients in that pestering and interruptive fashion, the grind will never end.

When you change the way you market, and begin attracting clients to you, you can create a massive amount of leverage. You can create a business that grows exponentially, while you work the same amount of time (or possibly even less).

The best part? You'll enjoy this form of marketing, and your clients will enjoy it too. You'll be doing things that are more pleasurable and enjoyable, for both you and your audience.

GETTING BACK TO THE REASON YOU GOT INTO REAL ESTATE

If you're like me, the reason you got into this business was to provide value to people. You're passionate about real estate and about helping people in the process of getting the real estate they want.

Money is a big motivator for some agents, of course, but that's not what brings the best agents into real estate. The bad agents might come in this way, when brokers focus too much on the monetary gains and promises. But that's what perpetuates the negative reputation that goes along with real estate: real estate agents are just in it for the money.

When the business of real estate is advertised this way, there's no real or perceived value being provided to the consumer. It's simply selling. You sell houses; you make money. Consumers know that you're there to sell their house and to contact you when they're ready to sell.

But no one wants to be sold, right? We all love to buy, but we don't like to be sold. That's why you've got to change that dynamic and change the paradigm of how you think about providing value to people.

WHO THIS BOOK IS DEFINITELY NOT FOR

Now that we've covered the needed shift in mind-set, I think it's important to say this: if you're in real estate sales, and it's 100 percent about the money for you, and you don't care about providing value to people, then this book is definitely not for you.

You can close it now; send it back to me, and I will happily refund your money.

And not only is this book *not* for you, but this industry is *not* for you either, and you're likely going to become a contributing factor to the negative reputation that real estate agents have. So if you're in it for money and money alone, please stop reading. And please stop selling real estate.

Part of the mission of this book is to create a growing community of agents who are working to change the negative perception of the real estate industry by changing the paradigm and processes in which we provide value to people.

To benefit from this book, you need to care about people. And caring about people means that you're ready and willing to provide value to those people in the way that they enjoy.

You must value service, and being a servant, over simply doing whatever it takes to "make the sale."

WHY AGENTS TYPICALLY HATE THE LEADS THEY BUY

Buying leads is a relatively new trend, and it's a terrible one.

When lead vendors steal your leads and sell them back to you, they imply that the leads they're providing are some magic pill. No hard work, no unpleasant marketing, just a few hundred dollars for leads who are interested in speaking with an agent.

The reality is that the agent still ends up with awful positioning and a complete lack of power. The agent still has to chase these prospects, call them, e-mail them, text them, or whatever else the prospects prefer. In doing this, the agent loses all the positive positioning and authority that attracts a prospect to an agent.

From a profitability standpoint, there are plenty of agents out there who are making a healthy profit on leads that they purchased from lead vendors. But again, this isn't about profits. This is about much more than that.

I can't say it enough: *how* you get your clients is as important as actually getting the clients.

You're chasing them and following canned scripts and processes for chasing these people into submission. It's a phrase that makes me cringe (and is perpetuated by bad sales coaches and gurus), but it's often said that agents chase people until they "buy or die."

When you think about it, this phrase is ridiculous, right?

It's no wonder that agents consciously and unconsciously resist these kinds of activities. Who wants to be the person who is chasing after clients until they "buy or die"? Not me. And not you.

There are other issues with prospecting in general, beyond this new trend of buying leads. When agents don't have an audience or platform or process for attracting their ideal clients, they're always desperate. And that desperation is why agents feel like they have to answer every phone call, every text, every e-mail, and work with any human being who shows any possibility of being a client.

In that state of desperation and poor positioning, there's an almost constant level of paranoia. Where's the next client going to come from? How soon will that happen? What if it doesn't happen?

The desperate agents end up working with people who no self-respecting person would ever want to work with. These are clients who don't treat agents with the respect and dignity that they deserve and who don't value their agents' time or efforts or expertise.

Sadly, a lot of these agents will end up complaining about their clientele. But the truth is that it's not the clientele's fault. It's the fault of the agent and all the people perpetuating the activities that result in poor positioning and desperation.

That's why the message of this book is so important to me. Once you shift this paradigm of positioning, and once you learn the skills to build an audience, it creates a peace of mind in you that is the opposite of desperation. It affords you the ability to choose who you work with and feel empowered versus being in a position of constant desperation.

YOU'RE GOING TO BE IN ONE OF TWO CYCLES

You're going to have a snowball effect in your business, in one way or another. It's going to be positive, or it's going to be negative.

The negative snowball effect will come from doing all of those miserable and painful things that we've discussed. The positive snowball effect is completely the opposite and becomes a scenario where the momentum works in your favor.

Either way, it's going to snowball. It's your choice.

If prospective clients know that you need them, much more than they need you, who is in the better position? They are. If you are desperate because you don't know where your next commission check is going to come from and you don't know how you're going to pay your electric bill or utility bill, who has more power? They do. They've got all the power and the authority in the relationship.

Most people won't necessarily abuse that power, but there are plenty of people who will either consciously or unconsciously abuse it because they're the one holding all the marbles in this situation. That impacts your happiness and peace of mind as an agent.

But if you've attracted them to you by providing value, by being informative and entertaining, and they choose to work with you because of how you've positioned yourself ahead of time, well, now you're the person holding all the marbles. You're the person in the power position. You're viewed as the authority, and they'll listen to you and respect you.

Let's say you paid for a lead, have chased the client, and gotten him or her to utilize you to purchase real estate. Well, if the client wants to go look at a property on a whim, and he or she is the one holding all the power and authority in the relationship, what happens?

You're going to go show the property whenever the client wants. It doesn't matter if the client calls at 6:30 and wants to see the property in an hour, and you're just sitting down to dinner with your spouse. What are you going to do when you have no power or authority?

You're going to drop everything and do it.

But if you're an agent in a position of power and authority, it's going to be the opposite. Here's how that conversation would go:

Prospective client: "Hi, Josh. You're selling a property we'd love to see. Could we see it soon?"

Josh: "Great! I'd love to show you that when our schedules work out. Right now I'm about to sit down with my family for dinner, but let's chat tomorrow about that property. If it's a good fit for you and your needs, then, absolutely, let's go ahead and schedule a showing for tomorrow afternoon or the day after."

Prospective client: "Thank you so much! We'll look forward to chatting tomorrow."

See the difference? Having control and having the feeling of being in control is a good thing.

We all want to feel some level of control over our lives. And if you're in desperation mode, other people have all the control. If they say they want to see a property tonight at 7:00 p.m. and they've got all the control, well, you've got to do it. You either do it, or lose them as a client.

But when you're the one in control, you can be confident in knowing that you can respond in the way we just illustrated. Something to the extent of "Hey, this sounds interesting, and I'd like to take the time to do a little research and make sure this is really what would fit your needs and what you are looking for. And if we both think it's a great fit, let's go ahead and schedule something at that point."

When you create an audience and a platform, it also means that it's okay to lose a prospective client who isn't a good fit for you. You can be at peace with passing on clients because you know you have a waiting list of people who want to do business with you.

When you're in control, prospective clients are going to follow your rules. They're going to look to you as the authority and the expert. They'll know that you're the person who has their best interest in mind, and they'll respect that.

When you don't answer their every beck and call, and you act as the authority that you've already established yourself to be, then they're going to respect that and honor it. And if they don't, no problem. It's fine with you, because you've got other clients who are ready, willing, and able to work with you—clients who will respect you and appreciate your authority and expertise.

You don't have to lose sleep over any one client because you're not in desperation mode. You're empowered and in control.

TRADING ONE RAT RACE FOR ANOTHER

Most agents get into real estate because they're tired of the traditional corporate rat race. Sadly, what they don't realize is that, in most cases, when they follow the old-school ways of marketing and thinking, they're just exchanging one rat race for another.

What's funny to me is that the Internet has been around for two decades now and yet so few of the coaches and gurus and old-school brokers have really embraced the fact that life is completely different now because of the Internet. This includes a difference in consumer behaviors and consumer expectations, as well as a difference in the way consumers choose who they want to do business with. It is all wildly different now, thanks to the Internet.

The traditional mind-set looks at the Internet as a threat. They say the Internet is disruptive to the old ways of doing things. Rather than embracing change and understanding it, the old school resists it all.

They don't realize that if they can learn to think a little differently and change their perspective, there's actually much more opportunity now. There's a way of creating much more leverage than ever before.

It's amazing to me how behind the times the real estate industry is when it comes to embracing the Internet and social media and changing the way they do business. It requires real change. It does not mean taking the same approach that one takes when door-knocking and cold-calling, and just doing that on the Internet. People call that "noise" now, and it's not acceptable.

I've had plenty of agents tell me that the Internet "doesn't work." They'll say something like this: "Well, the Internet and social media, I've bought leads from there and tried to push my business on there, and it just doesn't work. They don't convert. The Internet doesn't work."

Of course it doesn't work for them, because that's not how the Internet works. And it's also not how society works anymore. The old ways of blasting and shouting and begging and chasing do not work anymore.

Those agents are doing the same terrible things they've been doing offline and simply taking them online. Then they wonder why it doesn't work. Well, it's the same reason why those tactics don't work offline. They're shouting at people and chasing people versus attracting them.

When you figure out the better path, however, it's going to work in both places: offline as well as online. The principles that we're going to outline in the coming sections will work just as well offline as they do online. It's bigger than the Internet, or any channel.

It's about becoming attractive, being a person of value, and being the type of person who people want to invite into their lives.

The number of marketing messages that people see every day, compared to twenty or thirty years ago, has increased exponentially. That's a big part of why the old-school tactics are less and less effective. There's much, much more competition now for people's attention. The noise has magnified greatly now, and that magnifies the need to change the way you do business.

HOW THE INTERNET PROVIDES MORE OPPORTUNITY THAN EVER

The Internet and its social media sites carry a very powerful advantage that marketers have never experienced before. This advantage can be summarized by one word: targeting.

On Facebook, where consumers are currently spending a staggering amount of their time every day, you have the ability to get incredibly specific with the target audience that you're trying to reach. You can niche down to a very specific audience, provide valuable information to them, and be entertaining to them in a way that was not possible years ago.

Prior to the Internet age, demographic capabilities were much more limited. You could send direct mail to a specific subdivision, for example, but you couldn't send a marketing message to all the people in a particular zip code who own a home, who earn an income of $50,000 or more, who have pets and children, and who are gluten-free eaters. You couldn't target an audience based on anything more specific than their location.

But you can now. You can get so specific that it enables you to deliver a very specific message and create a level of rapport and affinity that was not possible previously. It's not easy, by any means. It requires consistent effort and work to do it, and the toughest part is that it requires thinking differently about how to market yourself and your business.

Most people aren't willing to do that. They want somebody to tell them what to do.

This program is a good compromise when it comes to that instinct. I'm going to tell you what to do in this program, but it still requires you to think about your business and to think about the exact type of client you want to attract.

Why? Because I can help you attract your ideal client, but I can't tell you who your ideal client is. You have to think about that; you have to decide that. Do you love working with first-time home buyers who are recently married? Do you prefer working with people who are downsizing?

Do you prefer working with real estate investors? Do you prefer working with people buying a second home in a resort town?

These are questions for you to answer. I can't tell you who the ideal client is for you, but I can absolutely tell you how to attract that ideal client to you.

I'll give you questions and things to think about to help you answer the question of who you'd like to serve. But, ultimately, you've got to do some deep thinking to figure that out. It's the most important decision you'll make, because you're going to build an asset around this decision.

ANOTHER REASON THE INTERNET IS AMAZING: INEXPENSIVE TESTING

Another reason why Facebook and social media have changed the landscape of marketing is this: you can see and test what's working in a very affordable way.

If you try a direct mail campaign, let's say, it's hard to figure out what worked. It's costly; it takes time, and it's hard to prove. You select a zip code, you mail a bunch of spammy postcards, and you wait for weeks to see if anyone calls.

Then you have to ask everyone who calls you, "Did you hear about me through a postcard?" Otherwise, you'll have no idea whether it worked. And then the question is are they telling the truth? Do they even remember? Who knows?

Compare this to a digital advertising campaign on social media sites. Facebook, being brilliant in their assistance to the marketers that drive Facebook's revenue, allows you to test your content and strategies for a very small amount of investment of time and money. Within a day or two (and in some cases only a few hours), you can directly see the results of your campaign on a very granular scale and improve upon it to create messages for very specific audiences.

On social media networks and the Internet in general, you can create content for a very small segment of your market and only put that message in front of them. You can target and then subtarget further. You don't have to put the same content in front of everyone and annoy the people it doesn't resonate with or apply to.

This is one of the new rules of Internet marketing. It's not just about annoying people; it's about surviving and growing your business online.

Once you start connecting, your attraction can go viral. It can grow exponentially with no additional effort on your part. When you're connected with the audience that you're trying to attract, word of mouth spreads online and offline, and you can really leverage that.

At that point, you can essentially put a magnifying lens on that audience and dramatically increase the positioning that you have with them. When people engage with your content on social media, the sites reward that. They'll give you more access to that audience, because they know it's mutually beneficial.

The value inherent in the social networks online is the same as the value of social networks offline. Offline, we provide value to our friends by sharing information that we think is valuable to them. We carry that behavior online, and when people online share our content, we get huge advantages in advertising and positioning.

But again, all of this is possible only if you've clarified the audience that you want to talk to. The audience that you know you can provide value, entertainment, and information to in some way. That's the key to getting people to share your content.

When you create content that is valuable, people who

don't know you and have never met you will happily share that content with their circle of influence. Why? Because your content is helpful or entertaining or valuable to their social circle.

HOW THIS LEADS TO A POWERFUL SHIFT IN MIND-SET

There are two dominant types of mind-sets: a scarcity mind-set and an abundance mind-set.

Most agents live in a place of scarcity and desperation, and that's why they feel like they have to cast a big wide net. They have to make sure that they're open to every possible opportunity for business. If potential clients express any type of interest in buying or selling real estate, the agents have to hound them until they "buy or die."

The abundance mind-set, however, centers on an understanding of the type of clients that you really want to work with—the type of clients who you get joy from working with. It's a narrowing of your target audience, but despite casting a smaller net, your chances for success are going up dramatically. It's a narrow focus, but there's a deep abundance of business there.

THE ONLY WAY YOU CAN ACHIEVE "EXPERT AUTHORITY" STATUS

When you take a narrow focus, it allows you to go much deeper in your relationships. Going deeper with your target market then creates a level of affinity and authority that I call "expert authority" status. This powerful status can only be achieved with a narrow focus and an abundance mind-set.

It's impossible to achieve this when you're casting a wide net and not narrowing your focus. Trying to be all things to all people is going to cost you a lot of money and time, and it's not going to work nearly as well as it would if you'd pick a target segment of that market.

When you narrow your focus, it's more profitable and enjoyable, and it's more fulfilling. It's fulfilling because you're actually able to do exactly what you hoped was possible when you became an agent. You're able to help and serve people on a deep and personal level and that feels amazing.

CLIMBING THE RIGHT LADDER ON THE WRONG BUILDING

Every week, I have conversations with agents who are attempting to navigate this paradigm-shifting process of focus and segmentation. At some point in the conversation, the problem reveals itself. Here's an example of how that conversation typically goes:

Me: "Well, who's your ideal audience?"

Them: "My target prospects are people who live in the greater Cincinnati area. They own a home. They're really motivated. They have good credit."

Me: "Well, are you a brokerage of four agents?"

Them: "No, it's just me and my wife."

Me: "Okay. Well, then, at the very least, we need to pick a zip code to target. It's probably the zip code that you live in yourself. Let's go deep with that audience."

And this is the point where resistance will typically reveal itself. Why? Because agents have been led astray by poor advice from traditional brokers and coaches. Their ladder is leaning up against the wrong building, which is the huge building that represents a huge market that is too large for them to become an expert authority in. You can spend years climbing that ladder, and you'll never get to the top of it.

It's easy to see that huge building and want to climb that ladder, because when you look at prominent agents on billboards and magazines, it seems like they've achieved mass success in a huge market. It seems like they have better revenues, more listings, and more fans on Facebook. And maybe they do have those things, but here's the catch:

In a lot of cases, that successful-looking person is miserable.

I've met many of these prominent agents with huge operations. To have such a broad focus and cast a wide net, they're overworked and miserable. They have to employ a bunch of people and deal with all of the ongoing headaches of that. And often they have to run a business that doesn't feel true to who they are.

The industry puts these mega-agents on a pedestal, and brokers tell other agents, "If you're not trying to build that kind of business, then there's something wrong with you." And then the brokers tell the agents that the way to get to that level of business is to grind it out for three or six or twelve months (or three or six or twelve years for that matter).

The problem is if you're like most people, your ladder is leaning up against the wrong building. If you really saw the pain that most of those mega-agents experienced in the past, as well as now in the present, you wouldn't want that kind of business.

Money and earnings are the other incorrect assumptions when assuming that mega-agents are happy and successful. There's a relatively new viewpoint that's starting to gain popularity across all generations: our time is more valuable than our money, and we want to do something that we can feel good about and that isn't simply profit driven.

Many of those big businesses and global corporations are so heavily profit driven that it drives a money focus throughout our society, but I think that trend is shifting now on an individual level. People are starting to question the assumption that more money is what will make for an enjoyable career and life.

Certainly, money and profits play a part in our happiness, but beyond that, agents should be constantly asking themselves, "Is this what I want? Do I really want to have a big brokerage with three assistants and five buyers' agents? Do I really want that kind of business?"

Personally, I've been in those situations before, and I would never want that for myself. Everyone is different, of course, but this is for sure: you've got to ask yourself these questions, challenge the assumptions involved, and make sure that a big brokerage is what you want.

Most people don't actually want that. Most people just want to help and serve their community in a deeper way. And that's what I'm going to help you do, both in this book and as a part of our community at **ClientAlchemist.com**. You'll learn the strategic and efficient way to build an audience that you can help and serve and ultimately become their trusted resource when it comes to real estate.

FOCUSING ON LESS BRINGS MORE OF WHAT YOU WANT

When I ask you to narrow your focus and targeting, you might feel like you're saying no to a boatload of business. But you're not. You're simply saying yes to a different source of your business.

Here's a great example from the classic marketing book *The 22 Immutable Laws of Marketing.*

A few decades ago, Coca-Cola was really doing well. They were kicking Pepsi's butt, beating them five to one in market share. Pepsi, instead of trying to fight Coke on a broad level, narrowed their focus. Pepsi decided to go with a campaign focused on the "Generation Next," investing their attention and efforts into the new and upcoming generation. It worked, and Pepsi closed within 10 percent of Coke's market share.

Even though Pepsi narrowed their focus, they weren't just serving that narrow market. What happened was they attracted many more people than they expected by resonating with one specific group. Even if people weren't in the "Next Generation," they still wanted to feel cool or look cool, regardless of age. Pepsi became attractive to a group of people, and that group of people attracted many more people.

It's absolutely counterintuitive, but trust me, a narrow focus brings abundance.

Maybe this will help you remember:

- Broad or Brand = Broke
- Narrow or Niche = Rich (and no I'm not just talking about monetary riches here)

You'll feel like you're saying no to a huge amount of potential business, but really what you're doing is making room for your ideal client to be attracted to you more easily. You're creating the kind of business you want and not putting up a false façade like the broadly focused mega-agents do.

You're becoming confident, genuine, present, and happy. And that's what will attract an abundance of people to you.

CONSISTENCY IS EASIER THAN EVER

When it comes to communicating with your target audience and publishing the content they value, the efficiencies of the Internet make this easier than it's ever been. And it's also more pleasurable than it's ever been on the consumer side.

As a result, you don't have to do all the old expensive tactics anymore, such as consistently sending out postcards or calling people. Instead, you can leverage the new technologies available, such as social media platforms and e-mail marketing. Using those tools, you can create very effective and inexpensive ways to communicate consistently with your target audience and deliver value to them.

The end product of your efforts? You create a deep, meaningful rapport with another human being in a way that can only happen through the consistent delivery of value. One of my favorite moments for me is when my students get this communication piece right and the results start to happen in a purely magical way.

It's that moment that an agent realizes that customers are now routinely reaching out to them, and the conversations go like this: "Hey, Jennifer, this is Jim. You don't know me, but I feel like I already know you because I've been reading your articles and watching your videos for several months now. Anyway, I'm ready to sell my house and buy another one. What do I do next?"

Compare this to chasing people down and how those conversations go. It's the exact opposite. Consistent communications will enable this for you, and the new technologies we'll discuss will provide the leverage to make it all happen.

THESE LEADS ARE HIGH QUALITY AND ALSO MUCH CHEAPER

Let me tell you about an agent named Kurt whom I've worked with recently. He's been able to apply this paradigm shift to his mind-set and strategy and has gotten some pretty amazing results this year. One of the ways to measure your results is by calculating your cost per lead and also by measuring the quality as far as purchase intent.

In the past, Kurt had been paying ten dollars per lead to a local mortgage company. But when he started utilizing the tactics and strategies we're outlining here, he was able to replace those ten-dollar leads with his own leads. What was his new cost per lead when he calculated the time and expense involved in acquiring each prospective customer?

It was under a dollar each. He reduced his cost per lead

by over 90 percent. That is absolutely staggering.

But it gets better. In Kurt's own words, these leads were "exponentially better in quality" than the leads he'd purchased in the past. This makes sense though, right? Because the new leads were chasing him versus him chasing them.

When he was paying ten dollars per lead, he was getting leads who didn't know him from a hole in the wall when he contacted them. It started on the wrong foot, and stayed there, in terms of power and influence. But now he's getting his own leads through his own publishing processes that we're outlining here, and those people already feel like they know him. They already trust him. It's just a wildly different perspective and experience. They're expecting his communication because he's gone from annoying pest to welcomed guest.

HOW DID HE DO IT?

First and foremost, Kurt started with the fundamental shift in perception and function that I'll continue to highlight throughout the book. He stopped thinking of himself as being in the real estate business and began thinking of himself as being in the publishing business.

Kurt focused on helping and serving his target audience with information and entertainment they valued. He didn't focus on selling them real estate, because that's not what the audience is typically looking for online.

There's a difference between these two statements:

Old: "I'm a real estate sales person, and my primary objective is to sell you real estate."

New: "I'm a publishing company that serves and helps this target audience in this target market. Also, although I don't talk about it much in my publishing, if anyone in that audience is ready to buy or sell real estate, they'll know that I can help them with that."

WHAT TACTICS DID HE EMPLOY?

Kurt was able build an audience on Facebook of three thousand people, and it's still growing *fast*. He was able to accomplish that over a period of only nine months. He posts interesting things to that audience (not just property listings), and they engage with him there. This inevitably leads to business, as Kurt stays top of mind for thousands of people in his target audience.

He's number one in sales in his zip code with his target

audience that he's serving this year. And he does zero cold-calling or door-knocking or any of those terrible things that he's probably been advised to do by traditional coaches and brokers. Instead, he has just focused on consistently communicating with the audience he wants to serve and attract.

He created a community on Facebook and a means in which to connect with them consistently on a daily basis. And in the very short window of nine months, he created an audience with real value. It's an asset with equity, and he's only scratched the surface.

If you'd like to read more about Kurt's specific tactics and strategies, as well as get his insights about the processes and their outcomes, I've added that information as a case study at **http://ClientAlchemist.com/BookExtras.**

ANOTHER EXAMPLE OF SUCCESS ON FACEBOOK

Paul is another agent I've worked with, and he also embraced the platform of Facebook and the mind-set of providing value through that platform. He wrote me an update after thirty days of utilizing the strategies I'd recommended for him, and he told me that those methods were bringing him business that would've otherwise slipped through the cracks.

In only thirty days of implementing the mind-set and tactics of providing valuable content, Paul had already generated the following results:

- Over two hundred likes to his Facebook page
- Over four thousand hits to his real estate website
- One home under contract
- One seller referral from that buyer of the home under contract
- Over 35 percent e-mails replied to him directly (from only one e-mail sent out to them)
- One new listing from his ads being shown on Facebook
- Ten new buyers who he reached out to and was easily able to set appointments with
- Many comments and likes on all of his ads
- Many people had even shared his ads with their friends
- Added Facebook advertising services to the portfolio of benefits he shows to prospective sellers

If you could have that type of result in only thirty days, wouldn't it be worth trying?

Here's the disclaimer though: Paul's results are no guarantee of yours. You have to take action, just like he did. You can't just think about it and hope that something happens.

CHAPTER TWO

Building a Better Mousetrap through Direct Response Marketing

· · · · ·

When people ask me what my company does, I describe it as "direct response Internet marketing." And by that I mean that it's a combination of inbound marketing and direct response marketing. To understand what I mean a little better, let's take a look at the Wikipedia definitions of those two concepts.

> **Inbound marketing** *is promoting a company through blogs, podcasts, video, eBooks, email newsletters, white-papers, SEO, physical products, social media marketing,*

and other forms of content marketing which serve to attract customers through the different stages of the purchase funnel. In contrast, attempting to purchase people's attention, cold-calling, direct paper mail, radio, TV advertisements, sales flyers, spam, telemarketing and traditional advertising are considered "outbound marketing."

Inbound marketing refers to marketing activities that bring visitors in, rather than marketers having to go out to get prospects' attention. Inbound marketing earns the attention of customers, makes the company easy to be found, and draws customers to the website by producing interesting content.

— SOURCE: HTTPS://EN.WIKIPEDIA.ORG/WIKI/INBOUND_MARKETING

Direct marketing *is a channel-agnostic form of advertising which allows businesses and nonprofit organizations to communicate straight to the customer, with advertising techniques that can include cell phone text messaging, email, interactive consumer websites, online display ads, database marketing, fliers, catalog distribution, promotional letters, targeted television commercials, response-generating newspaper/magazine advertisements, and outdoor advertising. Amongst its practitioners, it is also referred to as "direct response."*

— SOURCE: HTTPS://EN.WIKIPEDIA.ORG/WIKI/DIRECT_MARKETING

So the simplest way to combine the two definitions is this: you're marketing directly to your target audience, on all channels, and you're doing it with content that drives that audience to you.

You're providing value, being entertaining in some way, but then also mixing in ways that people can contact you easily. That's important, because sometimes agents can go too far on the other side with inbound marketing and customers don't know how to do business with them when they're ready.

That can be frustrating when an agent thinks to herself, "I'm providing all this value, and I'm doing all these things, and I'm not getting any new business from it." And in almost all of those cases, if you're really providing value, then the problem is that you're actually not making it easy enough for people to know what you do and how to contact you.

It's a happy medium. You can still get results when you're too far on either side of it, but if you really get that balance right, it's exponentially effective and even magical. If you can really strike this balance between inbound marketing principles and direct response principles, and do it by leveraging the Internet and social media, that's where the magic will happen for you.

EXAMPLES OF DIRECT RESPONSE MARKETING

In the world of real estate sales, direct response marketing techniques are typically involved in any situation where you're making an implicit call to action to your audience. So for our purposes here, it might be promoting a new listing.

It's important to keep inbound marketing strengths in play here by promoting your listing in a way that is interesting or entertaining or funny, or some combination of all. But from a direct response standpoint, it's incredibly important to include a call to action for people to respond directly if they are interested. And that call to action needs to explain how people can contact you and make it as easy as possible for the consumer.

The most common call to action would be one of two things:

- "Call or text at (555) 555-5555." Putting the actual number there is important.
- "Visit this link for more details about the property." Linking the actual link is important.

The key insight here is that you can't just have inbound marketing or direct response. You have to strike a balance between those two things, and you have to diversify how often you ask your audience to take action.

I have an 80/20 rule of thumb for Facebook, meaning that 80 percent of the time (or more) you're not asking for business or for any call to action. You're just providing valuable content. And 20 percent of the time (sometimes more, sometimes less), you're asking for business or for a certain action.

If you go too heavy on the direct response style of content and ask too often for your audience to take action for you, then you're just becoming part of the advertising noise again. You're becoming the noise and being seen as a salesperson instead of a value provider, even if you're doing it in a cool and interesting and entertaining way. It can still become noise.

THE NEXT CHALLENGE: RESPONDING TO RESPONSES

Later in the book, we will talk about how to respond effectively to people who have responded to your content and contacted you. This is another huge problem because you can ruin all of your hard work by responding the wrong way.

Once a prospective client starts a conversation with you, there is a way to respond incorrectly and repel them from you, as well as a way to respond correctly and strengthen the attraction.

It's very much like dating. You wouldn't ask someone to marry you during the first date, right? So don't do that in your business, either. We'll cover it more in an upcoming section called "Converse," but the fundamental takeaway is this: your replies and communications need to be consistent with the way you provide value in your publishing.

Incongruent and inconsistent behavior repels people, but consistent behavior attracts them.

BUT WHY DO COMPANIES STILL DO OUTBOUND MARKETING?

There are still plenty of agents and brokerages who send out marketing pieces that serve no purpose other than talking about how great they are, or how great their programs are, and how much real estate they've sold. I think of that as traditional outbound marketing, and to me, it's virtually dead.

So why are there companies and brands continuing to do this?

There are companies and individuals who have such a large budget, and an ego to match, that they continue to perpetuate this. It's a monumental waste of money, because their efforts and budgets could achieve much better results elsewhere.

Let's take the example of the traditional outbound marketing tactic of mailing postcards and compare it to the newer technologies and processes online.

With the postcard or mailing campaign, you won't be able to segment your audience much. If I wanted to segment my own neighborhood, it would be hard to mail postcards only to the people who have kids in elementary school, for instance.

Conversely, this is quite easy to accomplish on the Facebook advertising platform. And why is it so important to segment my audience this deeply? Because, again, our job is to provide the most valuable and relevant content we can provide. The more congruently I can speak to my audience, the higher the response will be.

So if I wanted to attempt this with the direct mail piece, my mailing would have to say, "Do you live in Lower Manhattan and have kids in elementary school? Then you have to see this!" That would be more effective than saying the simpler, "Do you live in Lower Manhattan?" It might still resonate with a reader a little bit, but not nearly as much as it would if that person had kids in elementary school. Do you see the difference?

The difference, from a content perspective, is a valuable

one. In this example, you could provide the audience with really good content like the following:

"Do you live in Lower Manhattan and have kids in elementary school? Then I can't wait to let you know about the new park that has just been planned for our neighborhood." It's just a wildly different level of relevance and therefore you'll get an exponentially better rate of response when you're able to focus to that level. And that's much easier to achieve online than it is offline.

As consumers, we all appreciate this level of targeting as well. It creates a better experience and a way of getting information that's valuable to us. What's frustrating as a consumer is the blanket, shotgun, all-sales-all-the-time approach.

Consumers once tolerated salespeople shouting at everyone, but those days are gone forever (thank goodness).

COMPARING COSTS AND MEASUREMENTS

Online, you can speak very specifically to the audience you're trying to communicate with. It's efficient and inexpensive, compared to the traditional offline methods.

With the postcard mailing, it's slow at every step. You've got to create the direct mail piece and get it printed. Then you could be talking days or weeks for the completion of those steps. But online, you can create your campaign and get the results from it in a matter of hours. You could create, pay for, execute, and measure twenty online campaigns for the time and cost of a single offline campaign.

The calls to action are also much easier online when it comes to consumers having the easiest path possible for reaching you. If an offline mailing asks a customer to get their phone, type in your number, and call you, that's twelve actions: getting their phone, inputting ten numbers, and hitting the call button.

In an online ad or post, likely viewed on a smartphone, it's only two actions: clicking the phone number and confirming that you want to call. Or if it's on a desktop or tablet computer, that person can simply click an e-mail address, instead of inputting it manually.

There are 90 percent fewer steps required of a person online, compared to offline. And that's part of the magic of these new online marketing platforms.

WHAT ONLINE PLATFORM IS THE BEST?

As of the time of this writing, I think that most people should spend the majority of their time focused on Facebook. It's commanding the highest amount of screen time currently with adults who would be in a position to buy real estate.

However, these platforms and networks are going to change over time, and there are always multiple platforms that you can leverage on some level. It will depend on who your target audience is and where they spend time. That's part of what we track and discuss at **ClientAlchemist.com**. We're on the cutting edge of online marketing strategies, and you'll always be able to join us online to dive in deeper and stay updated.

GETTING STARTED: THE FOUR PRINCIPLES

For the successful execution of the strategies we'll be discussing in the remainder of the book, there are four primary principles to master.

Principle 1: Identify

"Identify" refers to identifying your target market. This is where you'll need to get very, very clear on who your target market is and why you want to serve them. Ideally, this becomes a story you can tell that audience. It's the story that explains why that audience is who you want to serve, and that story will become a level of connection with the audience that is authentic and powerful.

This will help you connect with your target audience at a visceral level and in a lasting way. There has to be a real reason why you want to serve them, and it doesn't have to be something that is crazy or unusual. It just has to be a real story. A story that you can live and breathe every day in every action you take.

Principle 2: Attract

"Attract" refers to what you're going to do to attract that target market that you've identified and how you'll execute those strategies. We'll cover this in depth both in this book and online in our community.

Principle 3: Connect

With "Connect" we'll look at the different ways that you are going to connect with your target market, which is crucial to how you're going to attract them. Plus we'll walk through the "hierarchy of connection."

Principle 4: Converse

Lastly, "Converse," is a term that's really important to me. The word "convert" implies an event of conversion and represents the old way of thinking and marketing. But "converse" refers to a process of interacting with people. It's a process and a way of thinking about how to get into more conversations with people.

It's a stake in the ground and a statement that it's time to treat people as people, instead of looking at people as leads or "just a number."

If you make it your goal to get into more conversations with your audience and to continue those conversations, then the results will happen. The only logical outcome after months or years of conversations is that they're going to do business with you and/or refer business to you.

When you focus on conversations, you really are focused on being a servant. When you focus on "conversions" you're focus is on "making the sale." People *hate* to be "sold," but they *love* being "served." (Now that's quote worthy :-).)

CHAPTER THREE

Stage One: Identify

· · · · ·

To begin, we need to get crystal clear on the audience that we want to attract. The important first step toward clarifying your audience is to understand that this will require a counterintuitive way of thinking.

It might seem that narrowing your focus is going to bring in less business, but the opposite will become true for you. The more narrow your focus, and the more narrowly you can identify the person you're trying to attract, the more easily you will attract that ideal client.

Think of it this way: you're laying the groundwork to attract more of what you want and less of what you don't want. You'll have to have the ability to say no to business when you do this, because you'll know that everything will work out for the better in the long run.

I've been championing this idea for some time now, but most agents still default to a focus that is much too broad. They do this because they are afraid of not getting enough business, but a focus that is too broad is exactly what leads to a lack of business.

Think about it this way: if you try to be all things to all people, you end up being nothing to no one.

GOING FROM TOO BROAD TO JUST RIGHT

A recent example of how I helped a client go through this exercise and narrow his focus was through an e-mail exchange. I personally respond to all of my e-mails, which I feel like my community and subscribers really appreciate. I asked him the following simple questions: Who is your ideal audience? Who are you trying to attract? Where are they? What are some other demographic attributes they have?

His response was one that is all too typical and much too broad. "My ideal audience consists of homeowners in these four cities." It is possible, if those four cities were very small ones, that this would be a good start. But when I did some quick searching online, I found that his target audience was over two hundred thousand people. I know that he is a one-person team, and it is simply not possible for one person to serve two hundred thousand people well.

We continued to drill down further into this initial set of two hundred thousand people. After an exchange of more questions to identify his target customers, we were able to narrow it down to one specific town where the target audience was fifteen thousand residents. That number was a much better benchmark to start with.

WHAT'S THE IDEAL SIZE OF A TARGET MARKET?

For target market sizing, I typically use ten to twenty-five thousand people as a general rule of thumb. In some markets, as little as five thousand residents might be adequate.

So now that we're down to ten to twenty-five thousand people in our target market, what does that mean for this agent? It means that he or she can very congruently communicate with this audience in a way that builds affinity with them. And it's a different, deeper level of affinity. It's a level of leverage that would not be possible if we were targeting two hundred thousand people in four different towns.

When you're congruent and focused in your communications online, you're rewarded by the social networks and marketing systems. Your cost to connect and market to that narrow audience goes down significantly, while at the same time dramatically increasing your ability to connect with that audience.

TARGETING POSSIBILITIES THAT GO BEYOND GEOGRAPHY

The majority of agents will be able to identify their target audience by geographic area, and many times, it's the community they live in. However, there are many examples of people who target based on demographics that go well beyond a geographic grouping.

A client of mine lives in and serves a small community of six thousand homes. The uniqueness here is that the majority of these are second homes used as vacation homes. If she were only to target that existing audience, the existing homeowners of that area that she serves, it's likely not going to be enough to generate the volume of business that she's looking to achieve.

In her case, we needed to think about some different things that would attract buyers and sellers into her target market. Where are the people who are buying these second homes? Where do they live, and what are some of their characteristics that we can use to attract them in their primary market?

In working through this with her, we found that the majority of her buyers were coming from a densely populated metropolitan area. But in that case, if we were to target that metropolitan area, it would be about two million people! Therefore, we needed to narrow it down further.

Her situation is exactly why Facebook is currently one of the most powerful ways to implement the principles we are outlining in this book. On Facebook, at the time of this writing, we can really narrow down that audience demographic, primarily by using their interests.

We made some decisions based upon information she already knew: most of these folks are married, most of them have children, and most of them earn $100,000 a year or more. We can narrow it by those elements easily using Facebook.

We can also narrow by specific interests, such as an interest in vacationing or investing. We can narrow it by purchase behavior. The options for narrowing down the potential audience are almost limitless when you get into the Facebook Ads Manager dashboard and start utilizing it to narrow your target market.

In a case like that, you really need to sit down and think about what do you know about this individual person (besides where he or she resides) in a way that will help you create content that is congruent with that person's interests. You'll need to think about this and possibly do some research, if you're uncertain.

BEYOND ASSUMPTIONS AND RESEARCH: THE VALUE OF TESTING

Lastly, it's going to come down to just simply testing what works and what doesn't. In any case such as this one when we're looking at a market as unpredictable as vacation home buyers, you won't know for sure if your efforts will be effective until you test different types of content and messages.

Once you've done that, however, you'll have a massive competitive advantage over your local competition. You're thinking differently, and working smarter instead of harder. And the best of all is that it's nearly impossible for your competition to reverse engineer what you're doing. They've got to do all the work and analysis you did, but they won't know how to do it.

Even if your competitors do some form of introductory research and testing, most of them won't have the patience or long-term vision to take consistent action to achieve the end goal. By simply taking these actions consistently over time, you will outperform your competition significantly in the long run.

HOW TO DEFINE WHO YOU WANT (AND WHO YOU DON'T)

If you are struggling with narrowing down and getting clear on who you want to work with, it can be helpful to focus on who you do not want.

Give yourself permission to do this without judging yourself. Don't judge what comes up when you think about this, because whatever surfaces in this process is the reality for you.

Maybe you don't like working with first-time home buyers because you feel they're typically indecisive or fearful or just hard to work with in general. This is completely fine, because there are plenty of agents who actually like working with this market for the exact same reasons—agents who feel they can be motherly or fatherly in that process and are fulfilled by that.

Maybe you prefer to work with female clients instead of males, or vice versa. For the purposes of this exercise in targeting, there's absolutely nothing wrong with that. This is your business. You get to choose who you want to connect with and who you want to serve as a client.

But most importantly, from a marketing standpoint, this targeting is exactly what will help create the clarity and direction you'll need in order to attract that audience.

WHAT TARGET AUDIENCE DO YOU UNDERSTAND BEST?

If you're confused about what demographic you should be targeting, it's probably because you're not thinking about the demographic that you're actually already a part of.

If you don't have a compelling reason why this isn't your target market, then it's probably your demographic. This is the audience that you best understand and can relate to, in most cases. These are people who are in your community, who are of similar age, and who are of similar context.

If you can target the person in the exact audience that you're already in, it's going to be easier to attract that person because you are already that person. You go through the emotions that they go through, participate in the same activities, have mutual connections, and consume the same type of information. You are them, and that will be a huge advantage within your focused marketing strategy.

Football, for example, is a sport that Americans get really passionate about. So if you're an Eagles fan and you're trying to attract Giants fans, there's incongruence there. It would be hard to create affinity with them because there's that critical disconnect. It's not real. It's not personal to you.

THE IMPORTANCE OF YOUR STORY

Human beings are hardwired to understand and relate to stories and to build their behaviors and connections around the stories that resonate with them. Whether you choose your target market by geography, interests, or any other context, it's important to have a simple and clear story behind why you are who you are.

There has to be a reason in your story that answers the consumers' question of why. Is this agent like me? Why or why not? Does this agent really understand and empathize with me? Why?

The first-time home buyer audience is a great example. If you really enjoy working with that audience, it's powerful and effective to build a story around the reasons why this is true. You could have first-time home buyers share their stories of the positive experiences they've had with you, and your story could be that you love to help and serve that market because you see the joy on their faces when they successfully buy their first home.

An example with an older demographic could be similar. Maybe you had to help your mom or dad downsize in the past and that experience is the reason why you are now helping others do the same.

FAKING IT IS NOT MAKING IT

Your story absolutely needs to be true. It has to be who you really are, because your target audience will see through it if you're not being true to yourself. They'll be able to sense if there's not a motivation beyond business and beyond simply wanting to get that person as a client. There has to be more than that.

Faking it, and being all things to everyone, may have worked in the past, but this is a completely new world, and if you don't build authentic relationships with your clients, a competitor will.

The other side of this coin is your feelings. Again, we're talking about a strategy that is not only effective in attracting business but also provides you with an enjoyable and happy life.

HOW IT FEELS TO FAKE IT

When I was in college, I was a health and physical education student, and there was an annual convention for all the health and physical education majors. Every year, they gave an award to the student of the year, and I won that award.

The entire process of winning that award felt fake and worthless to me. There would be nominees from every school, and then at the conference, you would get interviewed on the first day, and the winner would be announced on the second day.

I can remember being interviewed and giving the answers that I thought the judges were looking for, but they weren't truly my convictions. It didn't feel good at all. It was cool to win the award, but it wasn't an award based on who I really was—that is, someone who lives a life that life that feels authentically good.

This happens in traditional job interviews too, where you might know the answers you're supposed to give, but if you don't believe in those things, you're going to feel unfulfilled in the end. There is going to be inner conflict, and it's going to create physical and mental stress for you on some level, if that's the path you choose.

If you fake your story and try to be something you're not, then you're not going to be happy in the short term, and you're going to have a breakdown in the long term.

Behavior that is inauthentic doesn't get you into the positive cycle, and it will absolutely keep you in the negative cycle.

WHAT DOES THE POSITIVE CYCLE LOOK LIKE?

When people adopt the four-step process in the book, it leads to this snowball effect:

You'll get the **clarity** of who you want to work with and what you need to do next. That will lead to **confidence** to create **content**. The content helps you **connect** with the prospects you want to work with and gives your prospects the opportunity to **converse** with you. As a result, you **close** more deals."

TARGETING WITH CLARITY: THE TALE OF TWO MARKETS

Let's compare a city to its neighboring suburbs. They may be geographically close, within a mile of each other even, but it's futile to attempt to relate to both of the audiences at once.

For example, when it comes to creating content they'd find valuable, it's incredibly hard to provide value to both groups. If I live in the city and I'm looking to upgrade in the city, I'm not going to rent homes outside the city. If a home is outside of the city, it doesn't matter how awesome that house is.

To the city dweller who wants to stay in the city, the thought process is, "Yes, I do want to move and sell my home. But I love the city life, and I'm definitely not moving to the suburbs. You can show me the greatest deal ever on a house out there, and I don't care. It's not relevant to me."

I could have the greatest photos ever, and the greatest videos ever, and the greatest description ever, and it won't matter if there's no congruence with my target market. Yet this is exactly how most agents market their businesses and create content.

Nearly every market has this same contrast when it comes to city life versus suburban life, or suburban life versus rural life. So you can't say that your target market is a city and a suburb unless you go deeper than that with some type of behavior or interest that is common across those places. Otherwise, pick either the city or the suburbs, but not both.

WHAT HAPPENS IF YOU CHANGE YOUR MIND?

Your target market doesn't have to stay the same forever. It can shift and evolve over time according to you and your needs and the market's needs. You may want to start serving a different segment of that audience because something has changed.

Another great capability in modern online marketing is the ability to target people who aren't currently in your target location, but would like to be. To make a sports analogy as an example, your target geography is the stadium you own. You have a home audience and you have an away audience. Your home audience is the people who are already there, and the away audience are the people who want to be there, but they just started looking at ways to get there.

The majority of agents are going to do the best by just serving their home audience, but it's very possible now to serve that away audience too. And, honestly, if you serve the home audience well, then you'll naturally get some portion of the away audience through the content you create.

The away audience will start finding your content because they are seeking information about your stadium, and your home audience is going to share your content with some of the away audience because they want them to come to the same stadium. That's the beauty of social networking.

A DEPENDABLE TREND: PEOPLE RELOCATE OFTEN

Every year, 15 percent to 20 percent of Americans relocate to a different home. Every five to seven years on average, they'll do it again. And the fact is, if you're connecting with a large enough set of people, you can count on a certain percentage of them to buy or sell real estate every year. You don't have to wonder about that aspect of it because that's a fact and a trend that fluctuates but never ends.

Instead, what we're trying to do here is make it so that when they buy and sell, when they're at that point of consideration, you are their logical choice to be the expert to work with.

HOW MANY CLIENTS DO YOU REALLY NEED?

Another helpful exercise in having the courage to market to a smaller audience is this: How many clients do you need to have to meet your financial goals?

Assuming that commission rates stay in the range that they've always been in, for most people, ten to twenty transactions a year will easily meet their financial goals. That's only ten to twenty people. So then, what do we need to do to get ten to twenty clients in any market?

Let's go back to that ideal market size range of ten to twenty-five thousand people. Using the low end of this spectrum, we'll take the ten-thousand-person market. Well, we know that fifteen hundred to two thousand of them (15 percent to 20 percent) are going to relocate this year. How many of those people do you need?

The answer is one percent. You can provide value to one percent of these relocators (and one percent of the ten thousand people, really), and if 99 percent of the relocators don't use you for their buying or selling, you still win. You only need one percent.

The odds are in your favor if you do the work of providing valuable content. In fact, you're likely going to get more than 1 percent. But if you try to market to everyone, you're likely going to get zero.

USING FACEBOOK TO NARROW DOWN YOUR TARGET MARKET

Facebook is incredibly valuable because of the ability you have to target your audience in the most narrow and specific ways possible.

Here's an example of just how powerful the targeting can be on Facebook. Not only can we target homeowners, but we can also show our content to people based on criteria such as the following:

- Zip code
- Income Level
- Marital Status
- Parent?
- Additional interests that signal alignment with your target market include
  → Luxury Brands
  → Sports (Golf, Equestrian, etc.)

→ Sports Teams

→ TV Shows and Other Media

In addition, Facebook is continually developing even more advanced algorithms based on predicting someone's next behaviors. For instance, one recent innovation is a segment of people who Facebook believes will soon be relocating, and that's very valuable for many real estate agents I've worked with.

For screenshots, videos, and updated examples of advanced targeting on social media networks such as Facebook, please see the resources page I've put together for readers of this book at **http://ClientAlchemist.com/BookExtras.**

CHAPTER FOUR

Stage Two: Attract

· · · · ·

In this stage, you'll answer questions that determine the type of value and content to create for your target market. It's this high-quality, high-value content that will attract your ideal clients.

Here are the four questions you'll need to answer:

- How are you going to attract and connect with your target audience?
- What kind of offers to connect will you make?
- What content will you produce monthly, weekly, and daily?
- How will you further differentiate yourself and be attractive to your target audience?

The best way to go about answering these questions is to block off an hour to sit down with a notepad and pen and write out all the answers that come to mind. There's no right or wrong here, and there is no judgment. It's important to write whatever comes out for you, and we can refine it from there.

I can give examples of how to answer these questions, but it would potentially be doing you a huge disservice. Why? Because you probably have your best ideas already inside of you. If I give you the examples, you might just think they sound great and try them for yourself. But if you think creatively with a blank canvas, it can be a real mind-opening experience and yield ideas that will work best for your situation.

At this point, I'll ask you to take thirty to sixty minutes to write down some potential answers your four questions. This is a very important step that cannot be skipped. As a reference, I'll give you some extended questions toward answering each primary question. Let's get started!

1. How are you going to attract and connect with your target audience?

What would you find interesting, valuable, and entertaining if you were your target audience? In most cases, you will be part of that target audience, so this should be easy if that's the case. But if you aren't your target audience, simply put yourself in their shoes and think about them consuming information online. What type of information or entertainment would they happily engage with?

Think about what type of content they would find valuable, informative, or entertaining (or some combination of it all) that they would be excited to get and consume. Content that would be a welcome guest, not an annoying pest. Content that is about them, not you.

This content does not necessarily need to have anything to do with real estate. Some of your content is going to include a real estate component, but some or most of your content is not going to be specifically related to real estate sales or topics. It's just going to provide value in the way of information or entertainment to your target market.

Write down at least twenty topics that you believe would be of interest to your target audience.

2. What kind of offers to connect will you make?

We'll dive more deeply into this in the next chapter, but there are multiple ways to connect perfectly with this target audience. Therefore, we need to have offers embedded into our content so that our target audience has a way to connect with us.

How will you offer to connect? What channels and social media networks do you spend time on and have a presence within? You need to give your audience an opportunity to connect with you in multiple ways and embed those offers into your content.

3. What content will you produce monthly, weekly, and daily?

You should have content that you produce on a monthly basis, content that you produce on a weekly basis, and content that you create on a daily basis. Think about what you could create in those intervals, that would provide value to your target audience segment.

Every agent will have a different answer for this question because how you provide value and inform and entertain is going to vary by who your audience is and what the theme of your content is.

For example, if you're targeting vacation home buyers or sellers, that content is going to be very different than the type of content you'd create if you were serving your local homeowners and community. Again, it's about making it about them and not about you.

4. How will you further differentiate yourself and be attractive to your target audience?

After you've put your audience first and determined what content to deliver, as well as how often to deliver it, it's time to think about your own strengths and personality and how to apply them authentically to your content creation.

It's crucially important that you are completely authentic to yourself, your beliefs, and your personality while delivering valuable content to your target audience.

One of my favorite compliments I receive on my content is when people tell me that I'm authentic. That's a great compliment to get and one that tells you you're delivering content in the way that attracts people.

The reason it feels that way is because it's true. I'm just being who I am.

I'm not trying to be something I'm not. I'm okay being who I am and knowing that some people are going to resonate and connect with my personality, while some people will not.

But remember the numbers? We only need 1 percent of people to choose us in the end. Even though we've narrowed down our focus, we're still not going to connect with that entire audience, and that's okay. We don't need to!

DO IT!

You're now ready to begin this exercise and answer all four questions. Please do not read any further until you have done this exercise, as it's a step that should not be skipped.

Remember, there are no right or wrong answers, and you can further refine this later!

FINISHED THE EXERCISE? NEXT STEPS

Now that you've finished your initial brainstorming, let's take the list of content and topic ideas you created in answering the first question. There will be at least twenty items on that list if you followed the instructions.

Next, write down on each line how often you think your target audience member would want to receive that information. Let's take the example of a real estate–related market update. If you're marketing to regular community members who only buy or sell every five to seven years, then those people are not going to want or need a real estate market update very often. This would likely be best as a monthly piece of content for this target audience.

After you finish that step, then you'll have a better idea of what pieces of content you'll utilize in offering to connect with people, and you'll be able to hone in on the type of offers you want to make.

Here's an example. Let's say one of the things you're going to do is create a monthly video to deliver the market update. In that scenario, your offer might be something like this: "If you'd like to get my monthly market update video right in your inbox, you can do that by clicking here." Your offer to connect is through the consumer subscribing to your video feed, and so you embed that offer within the video itself.

If it's daily content, perhaps your daily content will simply be on Facebook and focused on cool things going on in your target audience's community. It could be featuring a business, or talking about an upcoming event. It could be on Friday, maybe "Five Fun Things to Do Downtown This Weekend." It could be any number of these, but the way that you'd offer to connect on Facebook with daily content like that would be to embed the comment, "To find out more and stay updated, make sure to like our Facebook page!"

The offer to connect is going to be tied directly to the content itself, and the more smoothly that offer is integrated, and the more you put your target audience as the focus of the content and the offer, the more easily they're going to connect with you.

HOW WILL POSITIONING AND ATTRACTIVENESS HAPPEN?

If you execute the steps we've just walked through, your positioning and attractiveness will happen naturally. If you are consistently following your content creation and publishing schedule, and now you're someone who is providing value and being entertaining, people will immediately position you as someone of authority.

Naturally, they're going to see you as an authority because you're taking charge and being a leader through your actions. Agents who do this will very quickly start to feel like celebrities in their own marketplace because they'll start to be recognized when they are out in public.

I've been putting out content for years, and because of that, any time I go to an event, people recognize me and come up to me. Sometimes they want to take a picture with you. It gets that weird. But that's what happens when people feel they already know you and also see you as a market leader and local celebrity.

That will happen for you as well because you'll be taking a leadership position in your market, even though no one has nominated you for that. And you take that position by taking charge and providing valuable content to your audience on a consistent basis.

WHERE THIS CAN GO WRONG

People get excited about the idea of creating content to generate leads because it's much more palatable than the traditional alternatives of cold-calling and door-knocking and buying leads. But here's the catch: there's often no instant gratification.

Because of that, many agents get deterred or distracted. It's easy to understand why. Traditional real estate marketing has been pushy and fast. This new approach is genuine and slower.

Please, please, please keep going with this strategy until you see the tipping point: the point at which people start engaging with you online and offline in relation to the content you've created. And with advertisements especially, you can really get to a tipping point quickly and get into that positive cycle sooner.

When you cross the tipping point and people start to interact with you, you'll find it much easier to stick with your plan and continue to execute on it.

A friend of mine once made the following point on Facebook:

"Thirty-year mortgage, five-year car lease, four years of university, ten years of marriage, twelve-month furniture loan, but quits business in two weeks. See the problem we have here, folks?"

There's also a great quote from the marketing genius of Gary Vaynerchuk: "If you want to do something for the rest of your life, don't just quit after four months."

So if you're tracking with me here, and you really believe this works and you're buying into what we're talking about, then you just can't quit after a week or two. You really need to commit to this for success. It's a long game, not an instant gratification game.

THE OTHER MISTAKE: BEING TOO "SALESY"

Another way that agents can mess up this strategy is to be too focused on selling real estate. At least 80 percent of your content should not be related to buying or selling real estate. You should not be your audience's faces and pushy.

This applies to the mix of your content as well as the makeup of one piece of content. For example, if you do a market update video for your target audience, you want that video to be 80 percent content that they'll find interesting and valuable in some way. Then at the end, you can take the final 20 percent of the time to make them a simple and genuine offer to connect with you.

There's no perfect script for this, because it has to be what you're comfortable with. If you're comfortable with the offer you're making, it will come across as authentic, and it won't feel salesy to the viewer. But if you're working from some canned script, then it will feel inauthentic and salesy.

Part of the reason why real estate agents as a whole have such a negative reputation is because everybody is working from the same canned scripts. This is part of what drives the general population to get the sense that real estate agents are inauthentic and motivated by greed.

So don't contribute to that problem by using canned scripts or asking for business too often.

CREATE CONTENT FOR ONE PERSON, NOT A CROWD

When you create content, you want to create it as if you're talking to one person. You're not talking to an audience, but to an individual. That is received as more authentic and will help you connect with more people more easily.

This principle applies to all your communications, from social media to e-mail. Any content you're creating should feel to the end viewers like the content was created specifically for them.

WHEN WILL YOU HAVE TIME FOR THIS?

We're all busy these days, and you might be wondering where you're going to get the time each day to create content. That's a legitimate question.

The answer is this: it comes from the time that you spend thinking about doing the stuff that you don't like doing, that you probably end up not doing it anyway, and then feeling bad about going down the negative path into the negative cycle. There is a lot of wasteful time spent in the negative cycle.

So instead of enduring that daily nightmare, you just start blocking off an hour each day to create content for this strategy. And before long, this habit will become natural.

Does it seem intimidating, creating this content and publishing it? For some people, it certainly can be. If you're one of those people, then just create the content for yourself. Get into that practice, even if you've never really created content before.

If you've never done videos before, then just hit record and go. Start making the videos now, even if you don't share them with your audience, because this is what's going to lead to you becoming an expert. You'll become the person with the most experience, and eventually it will feel completely natural to see yourself on video.

This is especially important at the beginning. You've got to foster the habit and keep that habit going until you get to the tipping point. And to do that, you've got to set your content-creation schedule and keep it.

When you're doing this kind of marketing, it's important to create content consistently for the remainder of your career. But at the beginning, when you're trying to instill a new habit and get to that initial tipping point, it's the most important thing you'll do every day.

Make this a priority, and you will experience success in this strategy and have a massive advantage over your competitors.

WHAT IF MY BROKER SAYS I SHOULD BE MAKING COLD CALLS INSTEAD?

I've been there, and I completely understand. It's possible that in the short term, to keep your broker happy and to feel more secure, you may have to do those undesirable traditional tactics that help you survive. Your content creation may have to occur in addition to the tasks assigned by your broker.

Eventually, once your broker sees the results of your content-creation strategy, and sees clients calling you and e-mailing you, then your broker will understand. Your broker will want to know how you got to that pot of gold at the end of the rainbow.

WHAT CONTENT IS CURRENTLY WORKING THE BEST?

The most successful strategies in content creation are always evolving because the needs and behaviors of consumers evolve. To see case studies and further examples of content-creation strategies that are currently performing well for my clients, please visit http://ClientAlchemist.com/BookExtras.

CHAPTER FIVE

Stage Three: Connect

· · · · ·

We have identified your target audience and what you'll do as an agent to attract that audience. Now it's time to connect with them.

If you've executed the first two stages fairly well, there will be many different ways to connect with your target audience members. Ideally, you'll build things in such a way that your audience will take advantage of the unique attributes of your content and channels.

The first level of connection is one that most people don't know about. It's what I call the invisible connection.

HOW INVISIBLE MARKETING WORKS ONLINE

An invisible connection is created by an Internet file called a "cookie." A person visits your site, a cookie is put on their device (several cookies, typically), and then you get the ability to advertise to them again.

This has happened to all of us, whether we noticed it or not. If you look for a new pair of headphones on Amazon and you don't buy them, that cookie is on your device. Now when you go and log on to Facebook, it just so happens that in the right-hand side bar of your screen you see the exact picture of those headphones you looked at on Amazon. And of course, there's a link back to Amazon for you to buy those headphones.

It's a concept called "remarketing," or "retargeting," and savvy marketers in every industry are using it. And now, you're one of those marketers who understands the technology and will use it to help people get the real estate they want and need.

This is a new technology with new applications in the world of real estate sales. Just a short time ago, I wouldn't have advised this invisible connection, but now it makes all the sense in the world. I'm 100 percent in favor of doing this, and I think it's a key advantage. If you embrace it, learn it, and use it, it's going to make every other level of connection easier and stronger.

You'll be able to achieve those new levels of connection more effectively and at the lowest cost possible. The better you are at understanding this piece and executing it, the easier the rest of the connection hierarchy becomes.

THE HIERARCHY OF CONNECTION

In the hierarchy of connection, the goal is to take people from being in the pool of the largest group of people you'll be marketing to (your target market segment) and ascend upward into a stronger level of engagement and connection. The ultimate goal is not only to gain a client, but to gain an advocate who will refer future clients to you.

"ADVOCATE"

CLIENT

CALL / TEXT

EMAIL OR ONLINE INQUIRY

"FANS" (AND "FRIENDS" OF "FANS")

"INVISIBLE AUDIENCE"

THE TARGET AUDIENCE YOU IDENTIFIED IN STEP #1

After beginning by identifying the target audience you want to work with, the next level of advancement is taking this broader audience and turning them into your invisible audience that gets more targeted, repetitive, and valuable content.

This is accomplished through the cookies that are placed on the users' devices when they engage with one of your campaigns. We have a private client named Roger who, in the short time frame of six weeks, has created an invisible audience of 8,500 people.

For a minuscule investment of money and time, he has created a golden path toward achieving celebrity authority status within the market audience that he's targeting. I can't possibly stress enough how important this step is.

CASE STUDY: LUXURY NEW CONSTRUCTION SALES

Let's follow this concept within an actual example with screen shots that enable you to see exactly how it was done.

The agent in this example has a content-creation schedule that includes a weekly video featuring a new construction luxury home. It's a short video, normally only one to two minutes, but it's effective and consistent. It's valuable and interesting to his target audience.

The video is uploaded directly onto his Facebook business page (or "fan page"), and we promote that video. We run an advertising campaign that inserts the video into the news feed of his broadest target audience. This is the broadest-reaching target audience that is created first in the stage-one phase of identifying your target market. In this example, that market was roughly thirty thousand people.

After doing that consistently for seven or eight weeks, many people have engaged with that video, whether that's a like, or a comment, or a share of the video. And when that happens, the cookie is placed on that person's device, and that person becomes part of the invisible audience. This is the "invisible audience" I referred to previously.

In eight weeks, that audience had already grown to 8,500 people.

THE BENEFIT OF THIS NEW AND INVISIBLE AUDIENCE

Now that he has 8,500 people who were intentionally selected and targeted, who engaged with some of is content, he can continue to put more content in front of them. And they're okay with this, and actually even enjoy it, because it's done correctly and congruently.

They're already interested in who he is and what he's doing. They've proven it with the content they've engaged with in the past. This group of people will reengage and connect with him at a greater rate and for a lower cost when compared to his entire targeted marketed (and certainly when compared to any broader untargeted market).

Because they've been interested in his content, and they're going to be able to get more of it on a consistent basis, this brings the opportunity to create a level of rapport and recognition that was not available previously.

Accomplishing this in the past would have been tedious and expensive. An agent would have had to buy up every billboard in that target consumer's geographic area and then buy an extremely high amounts of advertising time on TV or radio to supplement the billboards and completely engage the target audience. But now you can accomplish this in a more effective and efficient manner online, and it's very inexpensive.

WHAT TYPE OF CONTENT COMES NEXT, AND WHY

From here, when we promote other content, campaigns, or offers to connect, we can present those offers to only those 8,500 people who are in Roger's invisible audience. We can foster the advancement of the relationship between

Roger and his target consumers and move into the next level within the hierarchy of connection.

It would be possible, but much more difficult, to take the initial target audience of thirty thousand people and get some of them to connection level 4, where we're trying to initiate a phone call. That could still happen, but it would be much more expensive and difficult to accomplish that without advancing through every step of the connection hierarchy from top to bottom of that inverted pyramid.

That's the process we undertake. We're always advancing the relationships in a systematic but natural way, while continuing to create valuable content for the broadest target audience. We continue to market to that audience in order to grow our maximum potential reach, and then we customize the content and offers we make for every advancing level of engagement.

The focus stays on two goals:

1. Connecting with more people for the first time
2. Connecting with our existing connections in a deeper fashion

We're consistently broadening the connection base (while still remaining targeted in the ways discussed earlier), and we're going deeper with our existing connections. We are always doing both of those things.

WHAT TYPE OF ENGAGEMENT CAN BE DRIVEN NEXT?

Once we've built this invisible audience, in this case, we want those 8,500 people to "like" our page on Facebook. It's our hub on Facebook, and we're going to leverage everything they allow us to leverage on that platform.

In this example, it would simply entail running campaigns that ask users to like the business page. It could be something as straightforward as, "Do you like (target city/area) luxury real estate? Then like our page." or "Own a home in (target city/area)? Then like our page."

The next action we'd like to drive is to get them to make an online inquiry to the agent. That's where our different offers are going to come into place. You need to have content that is valuable enough that a consumer would be willing to give their contact information to you in order to get that valuable content.

What type of content is that? That's for you to answer, because it's going to depend on your geographic market, the interests of your target audience, and what your business does and provides. In this example, it's a free weekly list of new construction luxury homes.

Again, because Facebook's ad formats change very often, we've built a page of resources at **http://ClientAlchemist.com/BookExtras** with up-to-date examples of top-performing ads.

There are many variations on this tactic of sending a free weekly list of information to people who sign up for it. You're only limited by your creativity and the type of business that you have. For example, you could offer a free weekly list of waterfront properties or foreclosures or investment properties. It's completely up to you and what your target market is interested in.

There are other ways to accomplish this as well, such as contests and prizes that aren't always related directly to buying or selling real estate. You could have weekly or monthly contests that relate to your target audience's interests.

Part of your content strategy might be to interview a local business, and when you interview them, you might team up with that business to create a special offer that is exclusively available to your subscribers.

In that case, your offer might be something like the following: "To get my weekly (target area) business owner spotlight and the special offer from this business, just enter your e-mail here. I'll send the offer to your inbox each week so you can be among the first to know."

Another example that's more closely tied to real estate is as follows: "Have you been thinking about what your house might be worth? Well, the Bob Smith Appraisal Company is giving away a $500 appraisal through this month's contest, and one person will win. Enter your e-mail below to qualify!"

IN TIME, YOUR LEADS WILL ALSO COME IN FROM UNKNOWN SOURCES

At this stage of your marketing, after you've been creating valuable content for months or years, it's also quite possible that people will skip all the levels of advancement in the hierarchy and simply call you out of the blue.

You can track almost all of the tactics we recommend on **ClientAlchemist.com** and gain a good understanding of what's working well for you. But there's an untrackable factor to this, in a very positive way, and in a way that will happen more frequently over time.

With almost every client I've helped with this process, if

they're consistently creating content and making valuable offers, they'll regularly get calls, and the people will say something like this: "I see you everywhere. I'm just reaching out because I'm looking to sell my home," or "We've been thinking about buying a home and you seem like the person to call."

You won't always be able to reverse engineer where this new client came from down to one campaign or tactic. And that's because it was the cumulative effect of doing all of these things that were valuable to that consumer and doing them consistently. It's really the sum total of all those things that creates this avalanche of business where clients begin appearing out of thin air.

Again, think about the difference in the positioning of you and your services when clients are calling you and asking for your help. Compare that to how the conversations go in the traditional methods where you're calling and begging that person for their business. It's dramatically different.

This person who is calling you is going to respect your advice, listen to it, and act on anything you tell him or her to do. And that's because they're looking at you as the market leader and expert, which you deserve, because you've done the things to position yourself that way.

This is the point I call "expert authority status," and you'll know it the minute it begins to happen. And if you are willing to take action on what we're outlining here, and you take a leap of faith, it will happen to you. And that's when life and business get really fun.

Once you're at this stage, you're in the strongest section of the positive cycle. You're going to continue to do more of that and be even better at delivering valuable content because of how good it feels to get business in that fashion.

OTHER TACTICS AND OFFERS THAT DRIVE DEEPER ENGAGEMENT

It's possible at this stage to run campaigns that promote a listing of yours, or perhaps multiple listings at the brokerage level, with the intent to drive phone calls or text messages to you. These types of promotions are becoming more common, so you'll want to see the latest examples we have at **ClientAlchemist.com/BookExtras.**

A word of caution: this is where the 20 percent of the 80 percent/20 percent principle would apply. You still want at least 80 percent of your content to be unrelated to your actual real estate listings and simply be interesting, informative, entertaining, and value-based content.

So if you do one piece of content that focuses on your listings and asks people to contact you, then you should follow that up with four pieces of content that are only focusing on what's valuable to the target audience.

You can still have some level of success if you're just posting listings, but there will be diminishing returns. The Internet is crowded and noisy, and people will gradually tune you out because you're just becoming salesy and noisy to them, like all the other salespeople.

But when you promote your listings in the right proportion, it is extremely effective. For every four or five value-based, entertainment-based, and engagement-based pieces of content, you can certainly mix in something that has a direct call to action. One example would be a specific listing, but you can see more ideas and examples on our website.

HOW YOU RESPOND TO PEOPLE IS IMPORTANT

The next level of connection, naturally, is an in-person meeting. It's naturally the ultimate result of your consistent actions in creating value for your target audience. For someone to become a client, there almost always has to be an in-person meeting, and how you handle that meeting is critically important. The next chapter, "Converse," goes into more detail regarding why.

In that chapter, we'll talk about how you can conduct your responses to people and your in-person meetings in a way that is more relaxed, effective, and consistent with the positioning you now have as the market expert.

People can do everything right when it comes to content-creation and marketing execution, but when those e-mails and texts and phone calls start coming in, they go back to the traditional behaviors (canned scripts, impatience, chasing people) and completely ruin the process and waste all previous efforts.

Forget about scripts. Forget about the idea of converting people. Here's the secret:

Just be a real person.

Simply continue the conversation. Treat potential clients like real human being. Treat them the way you would want to be treated.

If they ask you a question, then answer the question and ask them a question. If they reply to you, you reply and ask a question in return. I realize that this sounds simple and normal, but if you look at most sales scripts, it's not. Most sales scripts just fire questions at questions, thus driving a person unwillingly into an area of conversation that serves the agent, not the client.

But in this approach, and for the rest of your career, you hereby have permission to be a real person. You have now earned the right to continue the conversation in a relaxed and patient fashion, the way regular people would, until the logical end is that the client will need/want to meet you to continue making progress toward the outcome the client's wants.

Possibly that outcome is simply to go see a property, or possibly it's just a meeting to build trust. It might be at your office; it might be at a coffee shop. It could be anywhere, because that's how normal people meet and develop relationships.

It is refreshing, comfortable, and fun at this stage. Why? Because you don't have to know any secret sauce when it comes to sales and marketing. There's no script to memorize. You just need to be the caring human being that you already are.

RESPONSE TIME IS EQUALLY IMPORTANT (BUT NOT FOR THE REASONS YOU THINK)

When traditional agents buy their leads from the shady lead vendors, as I mentioned before, they have to respond to this lead quickly. That's because ten other agents have bought the same lead and will be calling that person soon to beg for business.

But in our approach, there's a different reason that you need to follow up with people in a timely fashion. And this time it's not out of desperation, or a fear of competition. You're the market authority now, and you're not desperate for business.

This is about treating people with respect and making their experience with you a positive one—an experience they will most certainly share with their friends, online and offline.

A RECENT EXAMPLE OF WHAT NOT TO DO

I am continually and utterly baffled by businesses that don't respond in a timely fashion, or even respond at all, when I'm trying to give them my money.

There's a local sports facility in my area, and I've called them four times in ten days in an attempt to rent their facility. I've left them four messages, and they have not called back at all. And you know what's crazy? I'm calling to rent the facility not once, but for the entire winter. In their world, I'm a potential customer who would be very profitable and easy to work with. And they have not called me back after nearly two weeks.

For our strategies to work in real estate sales, you have to commit to being the opposite of what that business is. Instead of being too busy to care, you're going to be the person who responds in a timely fashion and in a courteous and caring way. You're treating them like people, not like numbers or leads but real people who you respect and have empathy for.

If you do this, you will stand out even further from your local competition. And your advantage will snowball as you continue within this positive cycle. You'll create an army of people who will go out and talk about their very positive experience with you because that provides value to their friends too. Friends want to help friends, especially when it's something as important as buying or selling a home.

When you return calls and e-mails quickly, and do so in a caring and empathetic way, you are going to win clients over from your competition easily. It truly becomes easy.

THE SECOND BENEFIT OF TIMELINESS:
AVOIDING NEGATIVE BRANDING

Also important in our strategy, which hinges on online and offline reputation, is to prevent getting a negative reputation.

Let's go back to the example of the local gym facility I was trying to rent. Let's say after two weeks of not hearing back from Gym 1, I finally give up and start looking for other facilities. I find Gym 2, and they call me back immediately. It wasn't my first choice, but now that I have talked to someone from Gym 2 and have had a positive experience, it makes up for the fact that it's a mile further away.

Here's what happens next, from a reputation standpoint. The location and facility are going to come up in conversation, and I'll talk about my two contrasting experiences with all of the guys I coach with and play sports with. It will go something like this:

"Hey, guys, here's where we're going to be playing this winter, Gym 2. I called Gym 1 two weeks ago, four or five times, and they didn't call me back at all. But I found Gym 2 not much further away, and the manager, Jim, is awesome. He called me back right away and has set up everything exactly how we want it. I think we'll love this facility and definitely the management there, so we'll continue to use this facility for the foreseeable future."

See what happened there? One business got a positive reputation, and one got a negative reputation.

It takes some effort and action to earn a positive reputation, but it's your only choice, because if you take no action, like Gym 1, you're going to get a bad reputation with little or no business to speak of.

HOW MY GYM EXAMPLE APPLIES TO REAL ESTATE SALES

This example can be found often in the world of real estate, and it's especially noticeable in agents who have the mindset of looking at people as leads instead of looking at them as people who need helped.

Here's an example of why it's important to respond in a timely fashion and, perhaps even more importantly, why it's also important to treat everyone with a high level of importance and respect from the beginning.

Let's take two hypothetical people: Susan Starterhome and Megan Mansion. The names may be a bit silly, but hopefully that makes the example easier to understand and remember.

Let's assume that your target market is first-time home buyers of condominiums in the downtown area of your city. Susan and Megan are both looking for their first home in the downtown area, and they're equally qualified in that sense.

Susan Starterhome is interested in a $100,000 condo, and Megan Mansion is looking for a much larger $300,000 condo. Who do you think the typical agent would focus on and give more energy to? Megan, of course.

Luckily, you're no longer a typical agent, because you understand the power of helping Susan with the same care and enthusiasm that you'd help Megan. You understand that, because of social networking and the new world of online connection, every person you help can bring you a windfall of business. And you also understand that every person you ignore, or treat poorly, can put you out of business.

At the point when Susan and Megan reach out to you, you know very little about either of them. All you know at that point is the purchase price of the condos they're looking for. And based on that, you know that Megan's $300,000 condo will generate a commission for you that is 300 percent larger than the commission you'll get for helping Susan find a $100,000 condo.

But here's what you don't know at this point of first contact. And in fact, you won't know this until a year from now.

Megan, who will buy her $300,000 condo from you in a month, turns out to be a quiet and friendly person. She's straightforward, knows what she wants, and it was an easy and smooth transaction for you. She thanks you for your help and goes back to her business working remotely as a freelance computer programmer.

Susan, on the other hand, didn't buy the $100,000 condo she was looking for. You showed her several units over the course of the month and had some good laughs along the way. She was a really fun and social person, and she's a barista at the local coffee shop.

In the end, Susan decided that the condo association fees were a little higher than she expected and just a little too high for her budget, so she decided to keep renting. She thanked you at least ten times for taking the time to answer her questions and to show her the units she wanted to see, as well as for understanding her situation and decision.

Six months later, Megan is still happily working as a computer programmer in the condo she'll stay in for another five years. But Susan, well, she just landed a new job.

I know what you're thinking: now she can afford the condo. And that's true. She's definitely going to buy her condo from you, which ends up being $150,000. There's certainly the long-term benefit there for treating Susan well in the beginning. But that's nothing new, right? That's always been the case in real estate sales.

But here's what is different now in this newly connected online world.

Susan has a ton of friends. Not just from her years as a barista but also from being a social person in general. She's twenty-four years old, and as of the time of this writing, I can tell you that the average twenty-four-year-old person has 649 friends on Facebook. But Susan is far more social than average, and she has 1,452 friends on Facebook.

So what happens when she posts that photo of herself in her new condo smiling from ear to ear? Or tags forty-nine of her friends in the photos of her housewarming party? What happens when she thanks you for all your help and links your Facebook page to it all?

What happens is this: you just got introduced to Susan's 1,452 friends. And you didn't ask her to do that. Ten years ago, how long would it take for a person to physically tell 1,452 of their friends about you? A lifetime. But now it can happen in one day—in one minute, actually.

Ultimately, ten of Susan's friends become clients of yours, with an average purchase price of $150,000.

So which client ultimately sent you the most business? Megan and her $300,000 condo or Susan's $1,500,000 in referrals?

The lesson is a powerful one for today's reality. More than ever, you have no idea how influential a person truly will be in the beginning. You absolutely must treat everyone as a powerful, important person in this newly connected world, because that's exactly what they are.

Each person can single-handedly transform your business *for better or worse.*

I love that this is going to become a necessity in the modern world, because treating people in this way is not only good for business but also for humanity. It's the way we should all act toward each other as good human beings. We should give respect, empathy, and service to everyone we meet.

HOW TO GET MORE REFERRALS THROUGH BETTER COMMUNICATION

In the past, there was a mind-set that if you acquired twenty clients in a year, you would ask all of them for referrals to their friends and family. That worked to some degree, but it was just another form of pestering people, and it wasn't nearly as powerful as what can be leveraged within our strategy.

Today, you can create a form of communication that is authentic and real and connect with all of your clients in a completely nonintrusive way that facilitates their referral of you to others.

As a consultant to real estate agents, I end up on a lot of their e-mail subscription lists, and I get the same e-mails that they send to their clients. I see all the terrible ideas that have zero value, such as sending a "Happy Thanksgiving!" e-mail with a picture of a turkey. That's nice and friendly, but it doesn't engage me in any way or provide any value. It's not personalized to me beyond having my name filled into the automated form.

But if you send me a personal message in written or video form, that's going to engage me and generate positive results. Maybe you're talking about what you're thankful for, and you say that you're thankful to have me as a client and friend. And you finish by asking me a question about my Thanksgiving plans, or anything else that a friend might ask. That would be an authentic communication, and it would do a dramatically better job of encouraging a client to be advocate for you and to refer you to other people.

It doesn't take much time or effort, to market and communicate with people on an individual, personalized, authentic level. You just have to think differently, like a friend thinks. I think you need to be okay with sharing your personal thoughts and beliefs, as well as what's going on with your family. You need to do all the things that friends do, because when you do that, you create a level of connection that your competitors won't be able to compete with.

Share more of the things that are going on in your target market. Talk about why you love your community. Talk about why you love serving that community as a real estate agent, or serving in other ways. Share your thoughts and opinions and feelings.

As long as you're not sharing them in a way that would alienate the majority of your audience, they are going to resonate with your openness and authenticity. It's going to create a deeper rapport and relationship with your target consumers, as well as increase the likelihood of creating advocates who refer others to you.

COMMON OBJECTION: I NEED COMMISSIONS NOW, NOT MONTHS FROM NOW

When agents understand the value of this strategy, which is slower and more authentic and powerful, it's still not always easy for some agents. Why? Commonly, it's because this strategy feels like it will take too long to materialize into commissions.

One of my students was talking about this recently. He explained to me that his life situation had changed in a way that he needed to bring in more income and be even more of a breadwinner for his family.

But here's the odd thing that happens to all of us: he noticed that when he would focus solely on generating income, he would generally stay stuck. This makes sense, since our income is 100 percent focused on our needs and not the needs of our target audience.

Conversely, he noticed that when he would focus on the daily content creation and delivery of value, progress would happen. He went to Office Depot, got a big desk calendar, and wrote out how we was going to serve his target audience every day for the next four months. He understood this strategy and how he was going to turn that service into income, but his focus was on the service to others, not his bank account. He was focused on something greater than just the income, and that's why he was able to generate plenty of income.

I UNDERSTAND BECAUSE I'VE BEEN THERE

I completely understand how hard it is to shift your focus to the needs of others, instead of your own financial emergencies. If you're in a financially difficult situation, this strategy is easier said than done. And I get it, because I've been there.

There was a point in my life where I thought I was going to have to move in with my in-laws because of an unusually tough period financially. I wasn't just thinking about it or fearing it, but actually planning on it because it was days away from happening.

So I get it. I've been there. I understand what it's like to be in a tough place and how much faith it takes to change strategies when you're there.

But this is *exactly* the time you need to change strategies.

It's important to do whatever you can to take your focus off of your personal financial situation and put your energy into thinking about serving others. Instead of constantly focusing on how low your bank account is, the key is to focus solely on this:

How can I serve, contribute, entertain, and provide value to the audience that I am trying to attract? And how can I do it in a way that is consistent and congruent with them?

You can write that out on a piece of paper and put it on your bathroom mirror, or your refrigerator door, or somewhere so that it's always on your mind. This this is the thought process that is going to improve your financial situation, and it will happen faster than you expect.

The money will follow. It will. Money will flow naturally into your life because you've focused on providing the value that earns money.

HOW TO THINK ABOUT CONNECTING

You want to be viewed as a caring, giving person. And to come across as that type of person, you need to be that person. Embrace this role, but not as something you're doing to grow your business. Instead, think about it as your mission.

When it's your mission to be a caring, giving person, then you're past the mind-set that your competitors are stuck in. They're giving to get, being inauthentic, and it's obvious.

But you're different. You're not giving to get. You're providing value with no expectation of return, and yet in doing that, you will receive much more in return than you could ever imagine. The more value you can provide without asking for anything in return, the more you will receive.

MORE EXAMPLES ON OUR WEBSITE

Technology is changing very quickly, and our website will be the best place to keep up with the specific tactics and strategies that are currently working well for other agents. Below are links to resources there, which are updated continuously as technologies and tactics evolve.

There you'll find our most recent examples of campaigns specifically designed to build your invisible audience and active fan base, as well as communicate with them toward the next level of connection.

- Campaigns that drive online inquiries
- How to drive phone and text message inquiries
- Nine places to optimize your Facebook page for connecting

- Five fast and free ways to grow your following on any social network

These resources (and much more) are located at **http://ClientAlchemist.com/BookExtras.**

Stage Four: Converse

· · · · ·

In traditional marketing, this stage of the process would typically be called "convert," but I am intentionally using a different word that is much more congruent and effective for our strategy.

Converse: simply continue the conversations that have already begun.

If you will focus on having meaningful conversations with people who are reaching out to communicate to you, and you continue to provide value to them, then there is only one logical end: they will do business with you and refer business to you.

Again, this is the opposite of what most agents do. Most

agents are trained to convert at this stage and pummel the target prospect with some nineteen-point scripted language and push them into the agent's funnel at the fastest pace possible.

Instead of converting like those agents do, you'll be conversing in an authentic way. You'll be listening and answering questions to the best of your ability, as well as asking questions in return, like a friend would. You will be a better listener and provide value (being a servant) instead of being a sales person.

WOULD YOU GET MARRIED ON THE FIRST DATE?

It's helpful to think of this in another common scenario where important relationships are being built. Let's use dating and marriage as an example.

Much of the traditional mind-set for "converting" is driven by sales trainers and brokers who encourage you to do things that are the equivalent of asking somebody to marry you while you're still on the first date.

When a broker or trainer tells you to cold-call expired listings, or houses for sale by owner, or knock on random doors, they're telling you this: "Go get married today. And use this sales script to have the best chance of getting married on the first date. It's a high failure rate, but someone will be desperate enough to say yes, eventually."

Is this how you want to build relationships? I hope not, because it just doesn't work anymore.

With the thousands of marketing messages that we're bombarded with every day, and all of the ways we connect with people now, it just doesn't work that way anymore. It's now considered rude and inauthentic to be pushy. You can still get some business like that, but it's painful for you and for consumers.

But if you treat this process more like dating and courting, and getting to know someone, that will serve you well in this approach. Converse like you would on an important first date where you listen and you ask question. And you ask questions because you are curious about them, want to learn about them, and care about them.

This applies to every type of conversing, whether it's someone messaging you on social media, or sending an e-mail, or calling or texting. Treat every person like it's your first date with someone you want to have a second date with.

If you do, you'll easily and quickly rise above your local competition.

ATTRACTIVENESS THAT HAS STOOD THE TEST OF TIME

Religion and religious leaders are some of the greatest examples of value-driven relationship building in ways that have been continuously effective for thousands of years.

Let's take Christianity, for example. It's realistic to see that the Bible is one the greatest pieces of valuable content in the history of the world that is still being shared thousands of times on a daily basis. And its primary figure, Jesus, was the type of leader who was (and still is) massively attractive.

Why was Jesus so attractive to masses of people? It was actually quite simple: he genuinely cared about everyone. He told powerful stories and took powerful actions, and it was all built around genuinely caring for others.

That's it. And this is exactly the virtue that is attractive to every human being.

It's not only attractive to other people, but it's attractive internally. Who would you rather be: the person who tells stories and genuinely cares about others, or the guy with the headset on, cold-calling and pounding through the nineteen-point sales script?

It's an obvious question with an obvious answer. But in order for us to achieve this level of attractiveness and happiness, we need to make sure we're always taking the actions that are congruent with that answer.

Those actions always have one thing in common: genuinely caring for people.

CONVERSING THROUGH E-MAIL AND SOCIAL MESSAGING

We are all so inundated with information online that it's now very important to follow rules of engagement when it comes to responses to people. If you stick to the following three simple rules, you'll get more responses more often.

1. Keep your communications short and sweet, but with a conversational tone.

If somebody e-mails you and asks for more information about something, then simply answer the question. That person isn't asking you to tell him or her that you're a top agent in the market, or that you sold one hundred homes last year. The person simply asked a question and would appreciate a fast answer to that question.

Type your answer in the exact same way that you would write a response to your mom, or your brother, or your buddy down the street. If you wouldn't feel comfortable saying it to them, why on earth would you send it to someone you're trying to attract?

2. Convey a benefit (or potential benefit).

This will most likely or most often take the form of simply asking the person a question. So at this point in your response, you replied with a short and sweet answer to the question, and you've mentioned an additional benefit or a potential benefit.

3. Ask a Question in Expectation of Response.

Next, ask a question to which the person needs need to respond. Any response is good, because all we're trying to do is keep the conversation going until the only logical end is that the person becomes a client, or becomes someone who will send you clients. You'll keep going until you make sure that you have provided that person with all the value you can.

This is persistence, but in a natural way that is not pushy or overbearing, because it's consumer driven and not sales driven.

THREE SPECIFIC WAYS TO DIFFERENTIATE YOURSELF IN YOUR MESSAGES

Beyond the two primary principles of responses, there are

some specific tactics that also carry value in the modern era of relationship building online.

1. Your e-mails should come from you.

That sounds simple, but many people do not do this. They send reply messages from their brokerage or institute or investment group. Do not do that. Your messages should come from your actual name, Susan Smith.

If people are e-mailing you, they're e-mailing *you*. They're not e-mailing a corporation. And even if they do e-mail a corporation, they don't want a corporation to reply. They want a real person.

2. Your reply should look like "plain text" e-mail.

It shouldn't look like a fancy newsletter, or have a lot of computer code or graphics. This aligns with the core principle of keeping things short and sweet and conversational. You wouldn't respond to your mom or sister with a fancy newsletter template, right?

3. Be yourself and speak like yourself.

Write your e-mails the exact way you talk and think. This aligns with every principle in this book toward being authentic and genuine at all times. Never, ever, ever try to be something or someone you're not.

Think of all the ways it's repulsive to you when people try to be something they're not, both in writing and in life. It's not attractive at all, is it?

When agents try to be someone they're not, it's frustrating to everyone. Then the agent gets frustrated when clients aren't attracted to them. But it's the agents' fault. They should have just been themselves.

AN EXTENSION OF BEING YOURSELF: BEING CANDID ABOUT YOUR FEELINGS

Here's a common example of a stressful situation for a typical agent: an appointment request that would require you to miss an event that is important to your personal life. Let's say it's your son's baseball game.

If you miss your son's game for this appointment, what's going to happen? You're going to be mad at yourself, and you're going to resent the client who was responsible for this. But it's not the client's fault. The client will normally understand and be adaptable to your schedule if you simply tell him or her the truth.

The tone can be simple and honest and natural, like the following:

"Jim, I would love to show you that home and would love to work with you. My son's baseball game is tonight, and I made a promise to him that I'll never miss his games. I'd be happy to show you the property tomorrow afternoon, or Saturday morning. Does that work for you?"

What happens next? Most people will understand and adapt. But what if they don't?

Good. You do not want clients like that.

With that type of client, it's not going to get any better throughout the transaction. You're only going to become increasingly resentful of the client's demands, starting with the resentment you have from caving to his or her request early on.

You don't have to compromise on your personal values anymore, because you're now positioned as an expert authority. When you are positioned as a celebrity and authority, new clients will be more accommodating when you make requests. They'll do business according to your schedule and not vice versa.

Standing firm to your values will reaffirm your positioning as someone who is valuable and in demand, and it will keep you within the positive cycle of action. It will preserve your self-respect and your happiness with your career and life.

CHAPTER SEVEN

Facebook and Social Networks: What to Do and What Not to Do

· · · · ·

At the time of this writing, Facebook is the primary social network where people are spending the vast majority of their time online. There are 1.5 billion Facebook users worldwide and nearly one billion people log on to Facebook every day. In the United States, 20 percent of all page views that happen online are happening on Facebook.

This network is so big that it contains every age level, income level, geography, and behavioral segment. Your target audience is almost certainly there, and we want to meet people where they are. Therefore, we'll use a lot of examples and strategies for Facebook.

It's important to remember, however, that the world is changing quickly. Facebook may or may not be the dominant social network forever. With this in mind, every one of the principles we'll talk about will also be strategies that you can use universally on any social network or offline marketing platform. And as always, please refer back to **ClientAlchemist.com** to see updated examples for what's working well now.

WHAT NOT TO DO: EIGHT MISTAKES AGENTS MAKE ON FACEBOOK

We've discussed many principles and strategies about how to be proactive and genuine, so for this section, I'll take a look at examples of what not to do. It's often just as powerful to understand the wrong ways of marketing on social networks.

1. Leading with a brand name instead of a relevant interest.

It's tempting to make your social network hub the same name as your business. You'll see other real estate agents doing this in your market. But as always, just because they're doing it doesn't mean it is working, or that it's the best way for you.

Rather than leading with the name of your real estate company, it's more effective to create a page that is unbranded and focused on your target audience's interests. You want to create a theme and a name for your Facebook page, and ultimately additionally for your blog or website, that is about your audience and not about you.

So instead of Susan Smith Real Estate Services, go with South Charlotte Luxury Lifestyles. The unbranded name and approach will make it easier to connect with and engage with your target consumers.

When you lead with a brand, it just feels like another salesperson. It creates a negative association for most people in their minds, or at the very least, a cautionary guard. This becomes an obstacle to connection and engagement.

But if you lead with an unbranded message from an unbranded page, with a topic that's about them, they lower their guard and will more easily engage.

To me this is the most important of the eight mistakes, and I've been telling my students for years that they need to start with an unbranded means of connecting. Despite that, the majority of agents who bring me their marketing campaigns are still leading with business-branded pages. When you do that, you're fighting an uphill battle from the beginning.

Possibly, the desire to lead with your business name (or brand) is a hidden internal obstacle. I feel like it often comes from a place of ego and wanting to have your face and name and company get recognition. But again, this is the old way of marketing, and it will not be effective in the future.

When you see everyone going in one direction, you should really think about going in the other direction. And that's exactly what I'm recommending here. If you're trying to compete with the biggest name or brand in your market, you're going to go broke trying to catch up to them (and you'll be unhappy when you achieve their same level of high-volume, fast-paced misery).

Instead, you'll take a different path and genuinely connect with people. Soon after, they're going to ask you about your brand and your business. It should happen after they've connected with you, not before. If you try to do that before they've connected with you, like your competitors are doing, you're going to spend a huge amount of money and end up miserable. Guaranteed.

On the other hand, if your page is (for example) Northeast Minneapolis Homes and Lifestyles, think about how much easier that is to connect with from the consumer's perspective. And the reality is, even when people need to buy or sell real estate, they don't really want a real estate agent. They just want the end result.

We're creating an easier way for them to connect with you—an easier way for them to get to know you as someone with expertise in that area who cares about them.

A Typical Scenario: How an Unbranded Approach Works for Sellers
Here's an example of why this is so important. Let's say Bob comes home one day after learning his job will require him to transfer from northeast Minnesota to Texas. What is he likely going to do next regarding selling his home and buying a new one?

On the sales side, Bob or his spouse, Jennifer, will immediately contact you, because you've already built a relationship with them. They've engaged with your interesting and entertaining content related to the area, in part because you had a page that was not business-branded and focused on selling real estate.

They already know they're going to work with you because you've already connected with them and built a relationship, and you've never done anything to repel them. It's a foregone conclusion that they're going to choose to work with you to sell their house.

Even if Bob and Jennifer did not know you, it's becoming increasingly common for people to post to their social networks and ask for help: "We need to sell our house. Any recommendations?" And in that scenario, you'll get referred to them as well because you're viewed by thousands of people as the expert authority for real estate in that area.

The Next House: How an Unbranded Approach Works for Buyers
The second half of this example, and the side we haven't talked about yet, is what happens when Bob and Jennifer start to think about finding their next home in Texas. Social media has greatly changed this process in a way where this strategy works incredibly well.

Now back to the example and the day that Bob finds out he's being transferred. That evening, Bob and Jennifer each post a status update on Facebook, which reads something like this: "So sad to leave Minnesota, but we're heading to Houston! Will miss everyone here and visit often. Please come see us in Texas!"

Next, Bob's 457 friends and Jennifer's 862 friends see this update, and it turns out that one of Bob's friends knows someone in Houston named Howard and introduces them to each other through a Facebook post or message. These types of friend-to-friend introductions happen often in relocation situations. Why? Primarily because friends want to help friends.

The next day, Bob reaches out to Howard, and asks Howard about the area long before any real estate agent in Houston would know that Bob is moving to Houston. He asks Howard about the best neighborhoods and if there are any good sites or resources to look at.

What resource is Howard going to send to Bob? Bob doesn't need a realtor in Houston yet, and he's not asking for one. He just wants to know more about the area and neighborhoods.

So of course, Howard sends him a link to the Houston Luxury Lifestyles page. There's no reason to send Bob to a realtor's page.

And what happens if Bob later asks Howard for an introduction to a good real estate agent? Then Howard is going to send him to that same person, because that agent's content (on the Houston Luxury Lifestyle page) has proven its expert authority status and positioning to Howard.

Howard may not have actually met that agent, but will be happy to refer him because of the value that agent has established.

Social Networks Connect Value Providers, and You're a Value Provider
The lesson here? Social networks connect friends, and friends provide value to each other. Everything in this example is based on a friend providing value to another friend by referring that person to a resource that has proven itself to be valuable. And that resource is you.

2. Having a page that is not completely optimized for connection.

There are nine different places to optimize a Facebook page for better connection and engagement, and it's something we update at the aforementioned resource on our website at (**http://ClientAlchemist.com/BookExtras**).

Most people understand some of these, but very few people know or understand all of them and how to optimize them. One simple example is your profile picture and cover photo. Those are two pieces of media that you have on your page. The opportunity here is a powerful one: you can add a description to those images and give people a chance to connect with you.

Once you start attracting people to your page, they're going to start poking around. They're going to start checking things out and click on your profile picture or cover photo. You can and should optimize that description to create an opportunity to connect with your audience. Most people don't realize they can do this, and even when they do, they don't create a description in an optimal way to foster a connection.

This example is specifically about a Facebook page, but the strategy also applies to every prominent photo you have online, on your primary website, blog, or other social media channels. You want to make sure that your photos are optimized to create a way for your audience to connect with you.

Again, you might see pages that claim to be "optimized," but they could be totally over the top, asking someone to marry them during the first date. You don't want to do that. You want to make it as easy as possible for the person to connect with you, but also in the appropriate way that they're ready to connect with you at that moment and not try to force them into connecting with you on your terms.

You give them an opportunity to connect with you on their terms, and you make that as easy as possible. That's one key strategy to attract people to you and to inspire them to connect with you.

3. Lack of congruency.

In a Facebook ad campaign, there are at least five different opportunities to make your message as congruent as possible to your target audience. If you're not utilizing all five, it's a massive mistake and it's going to cost you money, time, and effort.

Let's look at a hypothetical example. You've created a post, with some good content or a valuable offer to your audience. Your target audience is a group of homeowners in the city of Mechanicsburg, Pennsylvania.

When we create this advertising campaign, there are numerous places where we can congruently communicate to that audience, both directly and indirectly, in a way that signals that this message is about them or for them.

One element would be the name of our page. If you're targeting Mechanicsburg homeowners and the name of the page is "Mechanicsburg Homes and Lifestyles," then you've already created one point of congruency and relevance.

Then, in the text of your ad, if you ask a question, "Do you own a home in Mechanicsburg?" or "Are you a Mechanicsburg homeowner?," now you've created a second point of congruency.

In the description of the ad, "This is a free service for Mechanicsburg homeowners," that's a third point of relevance and delivers an offer.

Lastly, the image of the ad is one that your audience would recognize and resonate with and instantly think, "That's my market."

If it's supposed to be about Pennsylvania, but has a picture of a Spanish-style home with a rock front yard and cactus landscape, it would be a huge red flag to the viewer. That would just be completely incongruent. That person will think, "This doesn't make any sense. He's saying Mechanicsburg homeowners, but that house looks like it's in Arizona. This isn't for me, or it's some kind of scam."

Again, this is critical beyond Facebook and in all your marketing. The more congruently you can communicate and craft your message to the audience that you're trying to attract, the greater the engagement and response your message will receive. The tighter you keep your focus, the better your results will be.

This is something that will only become more important over time, as the Internet and the entire world become even busier and noisier. As consumers are hit with a constant stream of marketing messages, the way to differentiate yourself is to be congruent.

If I sell an ad that says, "Are you a dad in Mechanicsburg who's frustrated by his boys not listening?," well that would stop me in my tracks compared to "Are you a dad who's frustrated?" I could be frustrated about all manner of things.

Do you see how different those two messages are to me as a consumer? The better you can do this, and make your message speak directly to the individual, the better your responses will be. You're not talking to a big group; you're creating a message for an individual.

4. Using stock images.

A huge mistake that so many people make is using stock images. Using Facebook as the example, they actually have stock images that they'll offer up for usage when you are creating and running your campaigns. But don't do this! You should never, ever, ever use a stock image.

It is critically important in all of your content that you have really high-quality imagery. It should be the imagery that you've taken yourself, or paid someone to take. It should be of your market. It should be congruent and resonate with the audience that you're trying to attract.

In one of our most popular courses, Audience Attraction Academy, one of the first homework assignments I give people is to go out into their market and take a minimum of thirty photographs of landmarks, marquees, signs, and a skyline. They are to take photos of anything and everything that their audience would recognize and resonate with.

When you do that, you will have a library of relevant imagery that you own the full rights to. You can use the images in your content and your offers, and it will make it all feel more congruent to the audience you're trying to attract.

Another Aspect of Photo Quality: Resolution

Another problem I see often is that people use really low resolution in their images. I am appalled, still, at the number of agents whose listing photos look like they were shot on a ten-year-old camera phone.

You simply can't do that without damaging your positioning in the eyes of your audience. Anything you put out is a reflection of you, so you want to put out media that speaks to excellence and not the opposite. That goes for Facebook, your blog, your listings, and anywhere else you have content.

It'll be a massive differentiator for you. If you have outstanding quality in your photos and videos, you'll differentiate yourself in your marketplace and really stand out from your competitors. If you're not interested in becoming a good photographer, that's no problem. You can very easily find talented photographers for a minimal investment.

It's worth the small investment of your money, because you'll create conscious and unconscious differentiation with the quality content that you're putting out there. If you've got poor pictures with a listing, it will be a poor reflection on you. That's hurting your brand, consciously or unconsciously, in the mind of the person who sees that. It's also not serving your client either!

5. Too broad an audience.
I've really tried to hammer this home because it is important in the beginning, middle, and end of everything you do. No matter how hard I try to emphasize this at all times, people still struggle with it, so I'm going to say it again: it's much better for you to go deep with a narrow audience than it is to attempt to be all things to all people.

Narrow it down, simplify, and identify your audience using the tools we've already discussed, and it will attract a broader audience naturally. Agents are afraid that they're saying no to business by narrowing down, but it's simply not the case. Your clients and invisible audience who are within your target audience will actually begin referring you to people who are outside of your audience.

If you're focused on your neighborhood, and you get a call from a referral who lives a bit outside your target area, are you going to say, "I'm sorry, you don't fall within the zip code that I'm targeting, so I can't help you sell your home?" Of course not. These referrals will come to you quite often when you do a great job of connecting with your primary target audience.

You're not saying no to business. You're simply focused on a systematic approach for attracting your ideal client to keep your efforts more efficient and effective.

6. Silly mistakes.

Double-check everything that you do, because silly mistakes can be costly and ruin a lot of valuable time and effort. Every time you're creating a post, or creating a piece of e-mail content, make sure everything works and does what it's supposed to do.

If you've got a link in there to your website, or a link in there to connect with you in any way, double-check that link before you send it out. I often get frustrated messages from people who say they followed my instructions, and I see that they did follow my instructions but made a silly mistake that prevented anything from executing them correctly.

Issues with linking are the most common problems. Sometimes the link is broken. Even worse than that is when a link isn't broken, but goes to the wrong page. If you've got a perfectly crafted message for Mechanicsburg homeowners and a person clicks on a link that goes to a page that says, "Hello, Philadelphia homeowner," then that person is completely rattled and thinking, "What? What happened? No, I'm not in Philadelphia." And in less than one second, that person is out of there.

Silly mistakes are straightforward. Just make sure your links are going to the right places. Make sure that you don't have any glaring mistakes in spelling. If you're doing an offer post that has your phone number in it for someone to call or text you, make sure your phone number is right.

Slow down, take a breath, and double-check everything. It's going to save you money and frustration and possibly even indigestion.

7. Unrealistic expectations.

You have to remember that this is the long game. This is not a push-button-easy game. If you expect to read this book, start taking action, and then give up tomorrow night because you didn't get a new client on the first day, that's the result of an unrealistic expectation.

Another similar mistake is to discount the quality of the results you get. I often get messages from people who say something to the extent of, "I ran this campaign on Facebook that you recommended and spent twenty dollars, and I only got three phone calls."

What's the problem here? It sounds like a great result to me!

You spent twenty bucks, you've got three people chasing you on a $300,000 house, and you're telling me this doesn't work? Maybe those three couldn't qualify for the $300,000 loan, but they're motivated and interested, and two of them have a home that they'd like to sell.

This sounds crazy that people would complain about getting three calls from $20, and it probably makes you laugh, but I get these comments all the time. What would you be willing to spend to get a client who is going to result in a $5,000 commission for you? I'd happily and easily spend $1,000. And this person just spent $20, proved the concept works (because three people called), and he is wondering why this strategy "doesn't work." Well, it *did* work.

We just need to remember what one client is worth and that we're not going to push two buttons and have commission checks in our mailbox tomorrow. We've got to be realistic about what it will cost, both in time and money, to get the connections that we're looking for.

One of the biggest benefits of our Client Alchemist Pro program is that we offer marketing critiques to all of our program members. If you've got a marketing campaign that you're planning to run, you can submit it to us, and we'll critique it for you and help you to improve it. You'll get realistic expectations on what will be achievable with your campaign, because we'll base our critique and advice upon what other agents have achieved with similar campaigns. We see thousands of them.

8. Cookie-cutter approach.

You can't simply take what someone else is doing, use their exact words and photos and ideas, and get the exact same results they got. Instead, you need to take best practices and principles, like what we've been trying to convey in this book, and adapt them to your business and the target audience you're trying to attract.

This mistake is born from the terrible advice of sales gurus and traditional real estate brokers. They give you a "one-size-fits-all" script, or maybe an entire website, and it's ineffective for all the obvious reasons.

FOUR LETTERS TO REMEMBER: VRIN

The best measuring stick to be used for determining whether a piece of content will be valuable is this: VRIN. That's an acronym for valuable, rare, inimitable, and non-substitutable. If your content and strategy pass all parts of the VRIN test, they've got a real probability of being valuable to your target audience.

If you're given a script for something that's a cookie-cutter approach, and it's something you can just copy and paste, how *valuable* is that? How *rare and inimitable* is that? How *nonsubstitutable* is that? Not at all. Cookie-cutter approaches have a very, very low VRIN score.

But if you take an idea or best practice, and you make it your own and tweak it and mold it to your business, it will be unique. The audience you want to attract will see it as valuable, rare, inimitable, and nonsubstitutable. You've simply got to adapt best practices to your personality, your business, and who you want to attract.

Conclusion

· · · · ·

When I was growing up, my family had a nursery and land-scaping business. I can remember, very vividly, spending my summer weekends and evenings doing all the grinding, hard work. That's why, from a very early age, I began to think about how I can do things in the most efficient way possible.

I was lucky because I was never told to go work for a set amount of hours. I was simply told to complete a task as quickly as possible. If they'd told me to go work for two hours doing a task, I probably would have mindlessly worked for two hours, and I might not be the person I am today.

But instead, I got into the habit of thinking about how all tasks could be best accomplished in the fastest way without sacrificing quality. Now, I affectionately refer to myself as "productively lazy," because I like to figure out the most efficient way to accomplish the end goal.

It's why I love innovative thinkers like Tim Ferriss. One of Tim's core concepts is minimum effective dose, which answers this question: What's the least amount of effort I can put forth to get the maximum result?

That's what this book is about. It's about working more efficiently and effectively so that you can feel comfortable working hard, because you know that you're also working smarter.

It's not working hard simply for the sake of working hard. It's not working hard because you're told you've got to go to work for eight hours.

It's unlikely that anyone in the world of traditional real estate sales is going to encourage you to work smarter, to innovate, and to think differently. Instead, they're more likely to tell you that you should spend three hours a day pounding the phones, cold-calling people. They are likely to tell you that that only feels terrible because it's hard work.

But this isn't why you got into this business. You got into

this business for the freedom that you can create for your-self. You got into this to help and serve others, to serve your community, and to help people realize their dreams of owning their own home. To help people achieve the American Dream.

This book is about helping you accomplish all of that in the most efficient, enjoyable, and effective way possible—to achieve it all in a way that you don't have to resort to demeaning yourself, or succumbing to becoming a glorified telemarketer, or feeling like a door-to-door salesperson.

This is for you, if you're the kind of person who knows, deep down, that there has to be a better way to do this—the kind of person who understands that the common and traditional marketing behaviors are not what you would want as a consumer.

This is the better way. This is the way you can work smarter and not harder.

This is the way you get to spend more time on the things you enjoy. And for most of you, that means actually serving your clients and serving your community. It means creating the freedom and the lifestyle that attracted you to this business.

This is the way that you become more attractive to your ideal client. You'll get to choose the clients you work with, and you'll have complete power over your schedule. You'll have the evenings and weekends off, if that's what you want.

You'll be the celebrity authority, the expert, and someone who will be listened to. You won't feel pressured to be at the beck and call of every potential client.

If this is what you want, then this is the strategy you need to take action toward. We have a tendency to want to wait until the timing is perfect, but that perfectly timed day never comes.

So that day needs to be today. Take a leap of faith and take action.

IT'S CONSISTENCY THAT WINS, NOT PERFECTION

One of the messages that I send often is, "Take consistent, imperfect action." If you take consistent and imperfect action, and you start applying what you've learned in this book, then you'll be slightly better at all of these strategies in one week.

In one month, you'll be dramatically better. Your mindset will start changing.

In six months, you won't be able to recognize the real estate agent that you once were six short months ago—the agent who wasn't taking consistent, imperfect action.

Kurt Nowicki, one of the case studies that we've talked about in this book, is a perfect illustration of this. Kurt has created tremendous success in the first nine months of using this strategy, and he's done it by taking consistent and imperfect action.

He admits that his actions are imperfect. He often updates our program members on his progress, and each and every time he says, "Look folks, I'm barely scratching the surface on implementing everything that I could be doing."

But he's doing exactly what it takes: consistent action every day. As a result, he's built an audience of over twenty-five hundred people in less than a year's time, and has become the number one agent in the zip code that he's targeting.

If you wait for everything to be perfect, you'll never take action. You have to be willing and able to simply begin.

If you don't understand something in this book, if it's not crystal clear, the fastest way for you to learn it is to simply begin doing it. When you start taking action, you'll start to get feedback from your target audience, and you'll learn quickly.

You learn through doing. You gain wisdom and knowledge through the process of taking action.

Go out and start taking consistent, imperfect action. And do it every single day. Block out thirty minutes of time every day to start creating valuable content for your target audience and begin implementing these strategies.

As you start getting results and feedback, you'll probably find it enjoyable, and it will be easy to block out more time for content creation. You're going to find it to be something that you look forward to, something that's fun for you to do versus the other traditional activities that you hate doing.

This part of your business will become fun. And the more fun you have with it, the more results you'll see.

CONTINUE YOUR JOURNEY AND LEARN MORE

If you're interested in more case studies, and the up-to-the-minute strategies that are working now, then I would invite you to visit us online.

As a reward for finishing this book, you've earned a month of free access to our pro community, and that's something we don't offer to the public. To take advantage of this incredible resource, go to http://www.ClientAlchemist.com/BookAlumni.

Acknowledgments

· · · · ·

I would like to express my gratitude to all the people who supported me in writing this book. First I'd like to thank Jeff Logue and Michael Smith. Without the two of you, Client Alchemist would not exist.

Next I'd like to thank Brad Kauffman who spent many hours listening to and organizing my thoughts into the book you are holding in your hands.

Additionally, I thank Andrew Lynch, Julie Stubblefield, Hal Clifford, and Zach Obront for their help and contributions to this process.

Finally, I'd like to thank Rob Minton, Ryan Fletcher, Dan Kennedy, Tim Ferriss, and Gary Vaynerchuk who have provided me with both direct and indirect inspiration for many years.

Thank you all!

About the Author

· · · · ·

JOSH SCHOENLY is the world's leading authority on digital marketing for real estate professionals. He is the co-founder of Client Alchemist, a company whose mission is to help real estate and sales professionals learn the skills and mind-set necessary to *attract* their ideal clients. This modern approach allows professionals to abandon old-school cold-calling, prospecting, and door-knocking. Josh is a devoted husband, father of four, believer, philanthropist, author, and freedom entrepreneur.

Made in the USA
San Bernardino, CA
03 October 2017